MANAGE YOUR EMOTIONS, UNDERSTAND
YOUR TRIGGERS, AND COMMUNICATE
BETTER TO RAISE HAPPY KID

PRACTICAL
ANGER
MANAGEMENT
for PARENTS

44 TECHNIQUES AND TIPS
TO BUILD A POSITIVE
PARENT-CHILD RELATIONSHIP

KRISSA LAINE

© **Copyright 2024 - All rights reserved.**

The content contained within this book may not be reproduced, duplicated, or transmitted without direct written permission from the author or the publisher.

Under no circumstances will any blame or legal responsibility be held against the publisher or author for any damages, reparation, or monetary loss due to the information contained within this book, either directly or indirectly.

Legal Notice:

This book is copyright-protected. It is only for personal use. You cannot amend, distribute, sell, use, quote, or paraphrase any part of this book's content without the author's or publisher's consent.

Disclaimer Notice:

Please note the information contained within this document is for educational and entertainment purposes only. All effort has been executed to present accurate, up-to-date, reliable, and complete information. No warranties of any kind are declared or implied. Readers acknowledge that the author is not engaged in rendering legal, financial, medical, or professional advice. The content within this book has been derived from various sources. Please consult a licensed professional before attempting any techniques outlined in this book.

By reading this document, the reader agrees that under no circumstances is the author responsible for any direct or indirect losses incurred because of the use of the information contained within this document, including, but not limited to, errors, omissions, or inaccuracies.

Free Bonuses

Thank you for your purchase! As a token of our appreciation, you now have exclusive access to five invaluable bonuses designed to enhance your understanding of Practical Anger Management for Parents and build a positive parent-child relationship.

Here's a glimpse of what you'll receive:

1. **Calm and Connected: Anger Management Workbook for Parents**
2. **Gratitude Unveiled: Cultivate Thankfulness, Unlock Serenity, and Transform Your Parenting Journey**
3. **Navigating Anger: Case Studies in Anger Management**
4. **Wisdom in Words: Nurturing Positivity, Transforming Reactions, and Finding Peace Within**
5. **Serenity Within: A Collection of Relaxation Exercises**

To access these bonuses, simply scan the QR code:

You can also access these valuable resources by visiting https://bit.ly/Laine-AM (Attention: The link is case-sensitive. Enter the link exactly as it is, with the correct uppercase and lowercase letters. Otherwise, the link will not work properly).

Support and Feedback

For feedback, questions, or if you encounter any issues, please visit the link or scan the QR code to share your thoughts and get assistance:

https://authorhelpdesk.com/support

Table of Contents

Free Bonuses 3
Support and Feedback 4
Introduction 7

Chapter 1: Understanding Anger 9
    The Nature of Anger 9
    Anger and Parenting 13
    The Consequences of Unmanaged Anger 15
    The Benefits of Managing Anger 16
    Myths and Misconceptions about Anger 17

Chapter 2: Identifying Your Triggers 21
    Personal Triggers 21
    Environmental Triggers 25
    Child-Related Triggers 28
    Relationship Triggers 30
    Health-Related Triggers 32
    Lifestyle Triggers 35
    Exercise: Identifying Your Prime Triggers to Anger 39

Chapter 3: Managing Your Emotions 41
    Self-Awareness 41
    Self-Regulation 44
    Building Emotional Resilience 47
    Emotional Expression 50
    The Role of Forgiveness 53
    Seeking Professional Help 55
    Technology-Assisted Anger Management 58

Chapter 4: Communicating Effectively 61
Active Listening 61
Conflict Resolution 64
Non-Verbal Communication 66
The Power of Positive Reinforcement 68
Instilling Boundaries 69
Exercise: "The Mirror Technique" 71

Chapter 5: Improving Parent-Child Relationships 73
Building Quality Time 73
Fostering Open Communication 78
Resolving Conflict Constructively 80

Chapter 6: Enhancing Adaptability 85
Adjusting to Changing Needs 85
Monitoring Personal Triggers 88
Maintaining Perspective 94

Chapter 7: Professional Help and Skills Building 99
Seeking Therapeutic Help 99
Anger Management Classes 104
Communication Skill Building 109

Chapter 8: Rebuilding Trust After an Outburst 115
Consequences of Not Rebuilding Trust 115
Techniques to Rebuild Trust 120

Chapter 9: Overcoming Setbacks 127
Identifying Lapses 127
Regaining Motivation 129
Building Resilience 135

Conclusion 141

Techniques Recap 143

References 149

Exclusive Bonuses 151

Introduction

At some point, every parent has felt that surge of frustration, momentary loss of control, and that flash of anger. This emotion is a part of the human experience, especially in parenting. *But what happens when those moments become more frequent? When the flash becomes a flame, and the flame begins to affect your relationship with your child?*

Anger itself is not necessarily harmful. It is a natural response to perceived injustices or threats, signaling that a situation may need to change. However, anger can lead to regret, conflict, and even harm if not managed appropriately. In the household, uncontrolled anger may create a tense environment for children.

The book **"Practical Anger Management for Parents"** offers valuable insights into an often misunderstood aspect of parenting: *anger management. Perhaps you question yourselves, "Why would I need a book on this topic when I do not consider myself angry?"* Recognize that experiencing anger does not make one an *"angry person"*; it simply means navigating a common emotional landscape. This book aims not to change your identity but to improve your emotional skills—particularly those that impact your role as a parent.

This book also provides a comprehensive guide to understanding and managing anger effectively. Drawing from psychology, neuroscience, and lived experiences, this book delves into anger's root causes and triggers and their potential impacts on familial relationships.

The book offers 44 actionable strategies for calming down in stressful moments, communicating feelings constructively, and resolving conflicts that deepen the parent-child relationship. It aims to empower you with tools for emotional regulation, not just for yourselves but also as a model for their children's emotional development.

Moreover, the book's scope extends beyond mere anger management. It promotes greater self-understanding, aims to improve parent-child relationships, and strives to foster a home environment where everyone feels understood, valued, and heard.

As you progress through the chapters, you will find this is not a critique of anyone's parenting styles or about blaming anyone. Instead, it serves as an invitation to grow, understand, and make positive changes in personal and familial life.

While some moments of self-reflection may feel uncomfortable, and some strategies may be challenging to implement, every effort, no matter how small, contributes to personal growth and a healthier relationship with the child.

Turning the page of this book could be the first step toward a new chapter in the parenting experience—one where anger is not just understood but transformed into a force for positive change.

Chapter 1
Understanding Anger

Anger is a universal emotion, not limited to those who display it openly or frequently. This emotion can sneak into parent-child interactions in subtle, often unnoticed ways, impacting your relationship with your children and their emotional development.

It is time to understand that your triggers and responses invest in your and your family's emotional well-being. This chapter is your guide to decoding anger and its meaning.

The Nature of Anger

Humans feel anger as a natural response to protect themselves from harm. When they feel threatened, their bodies release hormones like adrenaline, preparing them to either fight the threat or flee from it—the classic *'fight or flight'* response.

But anger is not always about external threats. Sometimes, it responds to internal feelings like frustration, hurt, or disappointment. It can be triggered by various events, from a child's misbehavior to a stressful day at work.

Remember, feeling anger is not the problem, but how you respond to that anger. Uncontrolled anger can lead to arguments, physical fights, work problems, and relationships.

The Physiology and Psychology of Anger

The body's physical reactions to anger, such as a pounding heart, flushed face, and adrenaline rush, are part of the fight-or-flight response. The daily stresses of parenting, like tantrums, backtalk, and perceived disrespect, can repeatedly trigger this reaction. Tuning into bodily cues like clenched fists is an early warning, allowing you to recognize rising irritation and intervene before reaching the breaking point. With practice, you can learn to pause, breathe deeply, and respond thoughtfully instead of reacting impulsively in heated moments.

Thoughts and perceptions can also influence anger. For instance, a child's spilled milk might appear to be done intentionally to provoke annoyance. Missed homework assignments could be misconstrued as laziness. However, beneath these expressions of anger often lie deeper emotions, such as disappointment over grades or embarrassment stemming from public outbursts. Parenting challenges can sometimes cloud your thoughts and obscure the more intricate emotional factors that underlie anger.

Self-awareness helps address root causes rather than surface reactions. Consider a child's backtalk, for instance. Rather than reacting impulsively with anger, it may remind you of your own experiences with childhood criticism. This recognition can trigger empathy as you remember your past emotions to understand better why your child behaves the way they do.

Similarly, when faced with risky behaviors exhibited by your children, understanding that these actions may be rooted in peer pressure and anxiety is pivotal. This awareness allows you to respond with compassion rather than judgment or anger. It further enlightens the psychological processes that underlie these behaviors, ultimately fostering a more harmonious family environment.

Developing emotional intelligence around your physical and psychological responses empowers you to manage anger proactively rather than reactively. This self-insight strengthens your ability to defuse intense emotions and make room for reason and empathy in your parenting.

Cognitive Aspects of Anger

The cognitive aspects of anger refer to the thoughts, perceptions, and thought patterns that influence how anger is experienced and expressed. The way you interpret and think about a situation shapes your emotional response.

For example, if a parent views their child's misbehavior as deliberately antagonistic, they will likely feel more anger than if they see it as developmentally appropriate. Thoughts like *"they are doing this just to annoy me"* generate more anger than *"they are still learning about rules and consequences."*

Some common unhelpful cognitive patterns that can exacerbate anger include:

- **Black-and-white thinking.** Seeing situations in extremes. For example, viewing a child's behavior as *"bad"* rather than understanding there are shades of gray.
- **Overgeneralization.** Making sweeping judgments based on single incidents. For instance, thinking a child *"always"* misbehaves when the behavior is occasional.
- **Jumping to conclusions.** Making assumptions without evidence. For example, assuming your child deliberately spilled their drink.
- **Magnifying or minimizing.** Exaggerating negative aspects or downplaying positives. Focusing extensively on a mistake rather than the overall effort.

Awareness of these cognitive patterns allows parents to manage anger more effectively by consciously reshaping habitual thought processes. While cognitive aspects contribute to anger, understanding them provides tools for change.

Emotional Aspects of Anger

Other underlying emotions can trigger anger. For instance, you might feel angry when you are hurt, embarrassed, scared, or frustrated. Anger often serves as a defensive mechanism, shielding you against more vulnerable emotions like fear or hurt. It is frequently easier to experience anger than to confront these underlying feelings.

Understanding the emotional aspects of anger involves recognizing these underlying emotions. When you feel angry, ask yourself: *"What other emotions am I feeling? Am I hurt? Am I feeling disrespected or unappreciated?"* Identifying and addressing these primary emotions helps you manage your anger more effectively.

To apply this understanding, practice emotional awareness. When you feel angry, take a moment to check in with yourself and identify any underlying emotions. Doing so helps you address the root cause of your anger and respond more constructively.

Behavioral Aspects of Anger

Anger expression is often a product of one's surroundings. If your upbringing involved witnessing anger manifested through raised voices or aggressive actions, you might mirror such behaviors in expressing your anger.

Engaging in these unconstructive or harmful behaviors, particularly when directed at your child, can have lasting negative adverse effects. Therefore, it is necessary to adopt healthier avenues for expressing your anger. Consider employing communication strategies like *'I' statements* to articulate your emotions, stepping away to cool down during tense moments, or utilizing relaxation techniques to mitigate your body's physical reactions to anger.

Put this into practice by paying attention to how you express your anger. If you notice unhelpful patterns, try to replace them with healthier behaviors. It might take practice, but you can learn to express your anger respectfully and constructively over time.

Anger and Parenting

Anger may seriously impact your ability to handle parenting successfully. You might react impulsively, resort to harsh discipline, or struggle to maintain an open and effective conversation with your child.

Chronic anger leads to a parenting style marked by hostility and inconsistency, which can be confusing and distressing for children. It can also create a tense home environment, where children may feel like they are walking on eggshells, always trying to avoid causing anger.

But remember that anger is a natural feeling that can signal that something needs to change. The real challenge lies in channeling this anger constructively rather than manifesting it in destructive ways.

The Impact of Anger on Children

Children possess keen emotional feelers, readily tuning into their parents' moods, including manifestations of anger. Consistent exposure to anger from parents can substantially influence a child's emotional and psychological health.

Experiencing recurring episodes of parental anger may predispose children to feelings of anxiety, dread, or depression. These children often grapple with diminished self-worth, internalizing the misconception that they trigger their parent's emotional outbursts. Over time, this can create obstacles in forging healthy interpersonal relationships and managing emotions and may elevate the risk of mental health complications.

Furthermore, children are adept at learning through observation. Witnessing frequent displays of parental anger, particularly if expressed through shouting, physical aggression, or other detrimental actions, primes them to imitate these behaviors. This perpetuates a generational cycle of poorly managed anger that may be hard to break.

The Cycle of Anger in Families

The cycle of anger within families can become a self-perpetuating loop. Unhealthy expressions of parental anger can provoke angry or negative emotional responses from children, which can cause further outrage from parents. This ongoing cycle can contribute to sustained tension and stress within the family dynamic.

Effective anger management can break this cycle. By demonstrating healthy ways to manage and express anger, parents set an important example for their children. This enhances parent-child relationships and empowers children with the emotional tools they need for constructive anger management and relationship-building in the future.

The Consequences of Unmanaged Anger

While anger is an ordinary and sometimes necessary emotion, it can lead to a host of negative consequences when it goes unchecked, such as:

Impact on Relationships

Consistent outbursts at home may create a tense atmosphere, causing loved ones to feel uneasy or fearful, eroding the trust that underpins a harmonious household. Meanwhile, in the broader social circle, including friends and colleagues, persistent anger can lead to conflicts, tarnish your reputation, and potentially jeopardize employment or friendships.

Impact on Child's Development

Aside from the emotional, social, and self-esteem aspects, the impact of parental anger on a child's development can manifest in other ways:

- **Cognitive Development.** Consistent exposure to a volatile environment can divert a child's focus from learning, leading to cognitive delays or academic struggles.
- **Physical Health.** The stress hormones triggered by frequent exposure to anger can impact a child's physical well-being, potentially leading to weakened immune responses, digestive problems, or sleep disruptions.
- **Coping Mechanisms.** Being in a high-conflict home can influence the coping mechanisms children develop. They may resort to unhealthy behaviors like withdrawal, aggression, or substance abuse to deal with their emotions or environment.

- **Attachment Issues.** Chronic parental anger can interfere with forming secure attachment bonds between parent and child, making it difficult for the child to form healthy relationships later in life.

Understanding the multi-faceted impact of parental anger can provide compelling motivation for managing it effectively for both parent and child.

The Benefits of Managing Anger

Learning to manage your anger can improve the following:

Improved Communication

Managing anger fosters improved communication and a more harmonious home environment. When consumed by anger, judgment is often clouded, leading to impulsive actions and escalating conflicts. Learning to manage this emotion allows you to pause, consider your thoughts carefully, and respond constructively.

For instance, when your child's actions trigger anger, mastering your emotional response enables you to articulate your feelings calmly. This clear expression can pave the way for a constructive dialogue about the behavior in question, its impact, and ways to address it going forward. Such open, respectful conversations enhance understanding and cooperation between you and your child.

Better Parent-Child Relationship

When you control your anger effectively, you create a safer, more predictable environment for your child. This can help them feel more secure and loved, which is essential for their emotional growth.

You also teach your child necessary emotional skills by modeling healthy anger control. They learn that it is okay to feel angry and that constructive ways to express it. Doing so can help them manage their anger and build healthier relationships with others.

Enhanced Personal Well-being

Being in command of your emotions means less internal turmoil and a clearer mind. This clarity paves the way for better decision-making, healthier interpersonal relationships, and a greater sense of inner peace.

Moreover, as you recognize and understand the triggers and patterns of your anger, you develop resilience against potential emotional pitfalls. This newfound emotional balance can liven your child's daily lives, infusing them with positivity and a deeper appreciation of life's big and small moments.

Myths and Misconceptions about Anger

As you understand anger, it is important to debunk some common myths and misconceptions that can hinder your progress. These misconceptions may lead to unnecessary guilt, confusion, and even resistance to managing anger effectively.

Myth: Good Parents Do Not Get Angry

The expectation that effective parenting equates to perpetual calm sets an impractical and damaging standard. Parenting inherently involves moments of stress, frustration, and anger.

Believing that *"good parents"* are immune to anger often results in feelings of guilt or shame, which in turn can heighten emotional reactivity. So, recognize that feeling angry does not make you a bad parent; it makes you human.

Myth: Suppressing Anger is a Sign of Strength

There is a common but misguided notion that *"strong"* individuals can suppress their emotions. However, suppressing anger rarely resolves the underlying issue and may have detrimental effects.

Unaddressed anger can surface in various unhealthy forms, such as passive-aggressive comments, lingering resentment, or even physical symptoms like headaches or digestive problems. Suppressing anger does not display emotional strength; acknowledging and constructively managing it does.

Myth: Venting Anger is Healthy

The idea that letting off steam by venting—*be it through yelling or physical aggression like punching a pillow*—will alleviate anger is misleading. Research indicates that venting often sustains the emotional fire rather than extinguishing it. It can reinforce neural pathways associated with anger, making it easier to trigger a similar reaction in the future. Controlled expression and constructive problem-solving are more effective strategies for long-term emotional well-being.

Myth: Children Should Not See Their Parents Angry

Shielding children from every instance of parental anger is impractical and a missed educational opportunity. While witnessing extreme and uncontrolled anger can be detrimental for a child, observing a parent constructively manage their emotions provides a real-world lesson in emotional regulation. It teaches children that anger is a natural emotion that can be handled appropriately, imparting important problem-solving and coping skills.

Myth: Anger Always Requires Immediate Action

The urgency that often accompanies anger may compel an instant reaction, but impulsivity frequently leads to regret. A hasty word or action can exacerbate conflict and negatively affect relationships.

Practicing restraint, even if it is just taking a few deep breaths or momentarily leaving the room, allows for a period of reflection. This pause can be invaluable for evaluating the situation objectively and deciding on a more constructive course of action.

Dispelling these myths enhances your emotional intelligence and enriches your family's emotional environment.

Chapter 2
Identifying Your Triggers

Certain situations and behaviors from your children may repeatedly spark your anger—constant arguing, ignoring household chores, and disrespectful language. These triggers may affect how you are as a parent to your children.

When you learn to identify the triggers underlying your outbursts, you gain control over them. You can anticipate rising anger and intervene early.

Equipped with this knowledge, you can remove those triggers instead of being ruled by them. This chapter explores how to identify your parenting anger triggers. Discovering your triggers changes anger management from reactive to proactive, empowering you as a calmer parent.

Personal Triggers

Personal triggers vary from person to person. Often, they stem from past events, personal beliefs, and physical states.

Below are some common personal triggers that can spur anger.

Stress and Fatigue

For parents, stress and fatigue can be potent triggers for anger. The constant demands of work, home, and family life can accumulate, stretching emotional reserves thin. When running on fumes, minor frustrations seem amplified. A toddler's tantrum or a messy room that previously warranted patience instead becomes the last straw.

Stress depletes the mental bandwidth needed for emotional regulation. A stretched-thin parent juggling work and home needs more energy to respond calmly to parenting challenges. Stress also heightens physiological arousal, prepping the body for *"fight or flight."* Parents become hypervigilant about perceived slights or disrespect that may escalate into anger episodes.

Fatigue, whether physical or mental, diminishes emotional resilience. Sleep-deprived parents often lack sufficient reserves to handle disruptions. Physical exhaustion saps the motivation needed for parental duties like engaging in play or household chores. Mental fatigue from constant multi-tasking hampers focuses, making it difficult to be fully present. This distracted, drained state leaves little room for managing frustrations constructively.

The combination of stress and fatigue creates a precarious environment where anger can thrive. Finding ways to mitigate their effects is necessary, whether through lifestyle changes, social support, or improved coping mechanisms. The path to anger management requires consciously addressing these energy-draining triggers.

Past Experiences

One of the less-talked-about aspects of parenting is how your personal history can trigger anger. While many parents are acutely aware of the immediate triggers—*like a child's disobedience or constant bickering between siblings*—less overt, internal triggers stemming from one's past can be equally potent yet more complex to identify.

For some parents, their upbringing can be a significant trigger. If you grew up in a household where anger was either expressed destructively or suppressed entirely, you might fall into similar patterns. Childhood experiences around discipline, emotional expression, and conflict resolution can often resurface, causing an emotional cascade you might not even be aware of.

Experiences of emotional or physical abuse, neglect, or other traumatic incidents in the past can shape how you react to situations as an adult. Such past traumas can make you more sensitive to experiencing anger or frustration when faced with parenting challenges that subconsciously remind you of these past events. For example, a past relationship marked by betrayal or dishonesty might make you overly sensitive to perceived lies or unfairness, triggering an angry response more quickly than another person might react.

Personal Beliefs and Expectations

Parents' beliefs and standards become anger triggers when reality does not align. Rigid expectations for behavior or family life often lead to disappointment and frustration when unmet.

Unrealistic Expectations Around Parenting

Many parents harbor an image of the *"ideal"* mom or dad who is eternally patient, always nurturing, and has endless energy. When the messy realities of parenting collide with this unrealistic expectation, it elicits profound disappointment and frustration. Falling short of an impractical standard makes parents feel inadequate. Rather than accepting occasional impatience or fatigue as normal, they judge themselves harshly, spurring anger inwardly and occasionally toward children.

Judgment of Child's Behavior

Parents frequently hold expectations around how children should behave—when to be quiet, how to interact socially, and what etiquette they should demonstrate. When your child inevitably contests these visions, anger often follows. Seeing a child talk back, throw tantrums, or forget manners makes parents feel disrespected. Rather than recognizing misbehavior as normal developmental tests of boundaries, parents perceive each incident as an affront needing swift correction.

Resentment Around Perceived Injustice

When one parent feels they disproportionately shoulder chores, discipline, or emotional labor for the children, resentment brews. They feel the burden of responsibilities is unfairly distributed, and their efforts are taken for granted. Frustration simmers, awaiting a trigger to erupt in angry episodes. The perceived injustice of doing more than their share eventually boils over, even if the other parent is unaware rather than opposing.

Judgment Around Deviations From Societal Norms

Anger can emerge when family dynamics deviate from societal or cultural norms. A father doing household chores traditionally seen as the mother's responsibility may unconsciously feel he is being judged, eliciting defensiveness. Parents who allow children more autonomy than is socially expected may be troubled by perceived scrutiny and doubts. Their anger shields vulnerabilities around bucking conventions.

Anxiety About Child's Wellbeing

As children act in ways that endanger their safety, success, or social standing, they evoke profound parental worry—and often anger. A child ignoring their gifts may be seen as wasteful, provoking anger tinged with fear about their future. Anger flares as a defense against intolerable anxiety that important values are being eroded or a child's well-being is at stake.

Environmental Triggers

In addition to personal triggers, your environment can also play a role in causing anger. Certain situations or settings can provoke frustration, stress, or injustice, leading to anger. Some common environmental triggers include the following:

Home Environment

The setting in which you live can act as a powerful catalyst for emotions, significantly influencing how frequently and intensely you experience feelings like anger. A chaotic, disorganized, or tension-ridden home does not just contribute to a heightened sense of stress and frustration—it can also lower your threshold for irritability, making even minor conflicts or disruptions seem far more aggravating than they might otherwise.

For instance, if your household is a hotbed of continual noise, distractions, or interruptions, it can always set your nerves on edge, leaving you more susceptible to impulsive outbursts at your children. Similarly, unresolved family conflicts or persistent arguments can serve as a simmering backdrop for your emotions, turning what might be minor annoyances into triggers for disproportionate anger.

Below are some proactive steps to cultivate a peaceful home environment.

- **Optimize Lighting.** Poor or harsh lighting can subconsciously heighten stress levels. Consider incorporating natural or soft, warm lighting to create a more serene atmosphere.
- **Declutter and Organize.** A messy home can serve as a visual and mental irritant. Dedicate time to decluttering spaces and keeping them organized, thus reducing unnecessary stress and frustration.
- **Mindful Decoration.** The colors and materials you choose can have a psychological impact. Opt for calming color palettes, soft textures, and nature-inspired artwork to evoke a sense of peace.
- **Auditory Environment.** Background music can significantly influence mood. Choose playlists that have a calming effect to help mitigate stress and create a tranquil setting.
- **Introduce Greenery.** Houseplants enhance aesthetics, improve air quality, and have been shown to reduce stress. Consider adding plants like lavender, snake plant, or aloe vera.
- **Designate a Relaxation Zone.** Having a go-to spot where you can unwind can be restorative. Whether it is a cozy reading nook, a space for meditation, or a unique chair set aside for relaxation, ensure it is inviting and comfortable.

Work Environment

Many parents juggle high-stress jobs, deadlines, and complex relationships at work, all of which can trigger anger and frustration. Some ways the work environment can become a contributing factor to parental anger include the following:

Interpersonal Conflicts at Work

Conflicts with colleagues, supervisors, or subordinates can evoke strong emotions, including anger. These unresolved feelings do not automatically disappear when one clocks out for the day; they often follow parents' home, adding an underlying layer of tension to interactions with family members.

Lack of Autonomy and Control

Parents who feel they lack control in their professional lives may inadvertently project these emotions onto their home environment, seeking to assert control in counterproductive or authoritarian ways.

Work-Life Imbalance

The intrusion of work into personal life—*be it through late hours, weekend work, or constant availability through smartphones.* A poor work-life balance leaves less time and emotional bandwidth for constructive, meaningful interactions with children, exacerbating stress and potential conflicts at home.

Social Environment

Seeing other parents who seem to *"have it all together"* can cause frustration and anger, particularly when you struggle with parenting challenges.

Feelings of isolation or lack of support can also exacerbate parental stress. The absence of a reliable social network for emotional and practical support can make parenting challenges seem insurmountable, triggering emotional outbursts as a form of coping.

Child-Related Triggers

Every parent knows that children, with their endless energy, ever-evolving personalities, and innate ability to test boundaries, can often push emotional buttons, sometimes leading to frustration and anger. Some of these "child-related triggers" are the following:

Child Behavior

Children, inherently curious and growing, often exhibit behaviors that can test the patience of even the most understanding parents.

Behind these behaviors lies a child's journey of understanding the world around them. Children constantly push boundaries as they grow to grasp societal norms, seek autonomy, and understand consequences. Their immature emotional and cognitive development means they often lack the nuances to express their feelings, desires, or frustrations.

Consider the toddler amidst a supermarket tantrum. They may be overwhelmed by sensory input, tired from a missed nap, or frustrated at being unable to communicate a desire. Similarly, a teenager's defiance might stem from the struggle for independence, peer influence, or underlying personal issues.

Such behaviors can be particularly challenging when you are dealing with your stressors, be it work, finances, or sheer fatigue. However, recognizing the developmental nature of these behaviors can offer a shift in perspective. Before reacting in anger, pause. Breathe. Understand that your child's actions, while exasperating, often are not personal affronts but rather explorations of their burgeoning independence and identity.

Child Development Stages

Different stages of child growth can also trigger anger. Each stage has difficulties and can test your patience in various ways. Understanding these stages can help you manage your expectations and respond more effectively when your anger is triggered.

Here are some common developmental phases that test a parent's patience:

- **The "terrible twos."** Tantrums, defiance, and limit-testing are normal but frustrating toddler behaviors. Understanding this stage helps you respond with empathy rather than anger.
- **Ages 5 to 7.** Children become more independent at this age, can talk back, and break rules. Remembering this is normal allows you to set reasonable expectations.
- **Preadolescence (ages 8 to 12).** Children at this age start pushing boundaries, demanding more independence, and having more significant conflicts with siblings. Planning for this stage prevents anger.
- **Teen years.** Rebellion, risk-taking, extreme emotions, and poor decision-making are common now. Recognizing these behaviors as developmentally appropriate can help you control angry reactions.

Knowing what to expect at each stage allows you to set realistic expectations and respond with wisdom rather than anger when challenges emerge.

Parent-Child Communication

Parent-child communication shapes the dynamics of the family unit. However, miscommunication or lack of communication can often trigger parents' anger and frustration. Here is a closer look at how and why parent-child communication can lead to feelings of anger:

- **Feeling Disconnected.** Parents might feel shut out if a child becomes withdrawn or stops sharing aspects of their life. This perceived distance can trigger feelings of worry, sadness, and often anger, especially if parents interpret the behavior as a form of rejection.
- **Generational Gap.** Different generational values and perspectives can sometimes hinder effective communication. What may be seen as *"normal"* or *"acceptable"* by today's youth could be foreign or unsettling to parents, leading to misunderstandings and conflicts.
- **Nonverbal Cues.** Misreading a child's body language or overlooking nonverbal signs of distress, unhappiness, or rebellion can escalate minor issues. When these cues are finally recognized, they might have intensified even more, leading to an angry response.
- **Perceived Disrespect.** As children grow, they develop a stronger desire for independence and autonomy. Their way of asserting this newfound independence might be construed by parents as defiance or disrespect, especially if the tone, words, or attitude feels confrontational.

Relationship Triggers

While relationships can be a source of love and support, they can also be a source of stress and conflict. These relationship dynamics can impact one's emotional well-being and trigger anger.

Marital or Partner Conflict

Marital conflicts add an extra layer of stress to the already demanding job of parenting. High-stress levels can shorten one's emotional fuse, making anger more likely in response to typical parenting challenges like discipline issues or bedtime struggles.

In some conflicted relationships, one parent's anger may lead to a competitive escalation, where each tries to *'outdo'* the other in expressions of frustration or authority with each other and their children. This creates a cycle of anger that can be difficult to break.

Differences in parenting styles can also become a source of ongoing conflict between partners. When parents are not on the same page, it can lead to feelings of resentment or frustration that intensify during parenting tasks, creating a volatile emotional environment.

When a relationship is strained, open and effective communication often suffers. Without a healthy outlet for discussing frustrations or disagreements, anger can fester and become a more reactive and destructive force in both the marital relationship and the parenting domain.

Extended Family Issues

Being a parent is not just about the relationship with one's child or partner but extends to a network of relationships within the family ecosystem. Extended family, comprising grandparents, aunts, uncles, and cousins, can play a role in a child's life. While their involvement often brings joy, support, and additional bonding opportunities, it can also lead to unexpected challenges and triggers for anger.

Some ways in which extended family issues become triggers of anger for parents include the following:

- **Differing Parenting Philosophies.** Older generations might have different beliefs about child-rearing based on cultural or generational perspectives. Unsolicited advice or criticism about parenting choices can be a source of frustration and conflict.

- **Boundaries Overstepped.** Grandparents or other relatives may sometimes overstep boundaries by making decisions without consulting parents or becoming too involved in the family's day-to-day affairs.
- **Expectations and Obligations.** Expectations of attending extended family events or adhering to certain traditions may exist. Balancing these expectations with one's family's needs and desires can be a source of stress and conflict.
- **Dynamics Around In-Laws.** For many, the relationship with in-laws is complex. Differences in culture, values, or interpersonal dynamics can lead to misunderstandings. Parents might need to defend their partner against perceived slights, adding another layer to the emotional mix.

Health-Related Triggers

Juggling the multiple demands of family life, work, and personal well-being leads parents to overlook health. However, physical and mental health are intricately tied to emotional responses, including the experience and expression of anger.

The following are health issues making the road to anger a shorter trip.

Chronic Pain or Illness

Managing chronic pain or illness is emotionally taxing. The continual cycle of doctor visits, medication schedules, and perhaps even surgeries can wear down your emotional reserves.

Chronic conditions often bring limitations that can drastically change your lifestyle, perhaps restricting physical activities you used to enjoy or requiring changes in work or social life. These limitations can create a sense of loss of control and shift in your identity, which can be frustrating and frightening—feelings that can easily manifest as anger.

Besides that, chronic pain or illness affects you and your family. Seeing them struggle or make sacrifices because of your condition can evoke feelings of guilt or helplessness, another emotional route to anger. Conversely, you may also feel resentful if you perceive a lack of understanding or support from your family members.

Research suggests that anger and pain are interlinked; each can intensify the other. Anger can heighten the perception of pain, which cycles back into anger. Breaking this loop often requires targeted strategies that address physical pain and emotional tumult.

Mental Health Issues

Sometimes, the origins of anger lie within existing mental health conditions, which can serve as triggers. Here is a closer look at how various mental health issues can provoke or exacerbate anger in parents:

- **Depression.** Anger is a less recognized but frequent symptom of depression. Parents who are depressed might experience low energy and increased irritability, causing less tolerance for children's natural, unpredictable behaviors. What might typically be an inconsequential incident can become a tipping point, escalating into outbursts of anger.
- **Bipolar Disorder.** The mood swings associated with bipolar disorder can also manifest as volatile shifts in temper. During manic phases, parents may feel invincible, making impulsive choices without considering the consequences, including angry outbursts. During depressive phases, irritability and frustration can likewise escalate quickly into anger.

- **ADHD (Attention-Deficit/Hyperactivity Disorder).** Parents with ADHD may find it challenging to manage the persistent demands of parenting due to difficulties with focus and organization. The consequent stress and feelings of inadequacy can lead to irritability and anger, especially when parenting tasks become overwhelming.
- **Post-Traumatic Stress Disorder (PTSD).** Parents who have experienced traumatic events may have emotional triggers that children unknowingly activate. For example, a loud noise or sudden movement might induce a stress response, triggering irritability or an angry reaction due to the parent's heightened state of alertness.
- **Borderline Personality Disorder (BPD).** Parents with BPD may experience intense mood swings and have difficulty regulating their emotions, including anger. Their emotional responses can be unpredictable and disproportionately intense, potentially creating a chaotic emotional environment for children.

Medication Side Effects

Some medications can have psychological side effects that may make you more susceptible to feelings of frustration, irritability, or anger. Understanding this connection is necessary, especially for parents already navigating the emotionally complex landscape of raising children.

The types of medications that can contribute to anger include the following:

- **Antidepressants.** While intended to manage mood disorders, some people experience irritability as a side effect.
- **Stimulants.** Medications prescribed for ADHD and certain other conditions can lead to emotional volatility, including bursts of anger.

- **Hormonal medications.** Birth control pills, hormone replacement therapies, or steroids can significantly affect mood.
- **Blood Pressure Medications.** Some beta-blockers are known for affecting mood.

These medications often alter the balance of neurotransmitters or hormones in the brain, which can impact emotional regulation.

Parents are already subject to many external pressures and triggers. Medication-induced irritability can exacerbate these issues, making minor irritations seem disproportionately infuriating and leading to situations where anger becomes challenging to manage effectively.

Lifestyle Triggers

Habits, choices, and daily rituals—*from the amount of sleep you get to the foods you consume or even the digital devices you are tethered to*—each element can act as a trigger. Understanding how lifestyle factors come into play can be particularly enlightening in the context of anger, paving the way for healthier responses and a more balanced life.

Nutrition's Impact on Mood and Emotions

What you eat directly affects your brain chemistry and, consequently, your emotions. While there is no *"miracle food"* that can eliminate negative emotions, certain dietary choices can help create a balanced emotional landscape. Some foods and nutritional tips that can support a good mood and potentially help with managing anger include the following:

- **Omega-3 Fatty Acids.** Foods rich in omega-3 fatty acids, such as salmon, walnuts, and flaxseeds, have been shown to help reduce irritability and mood swings. Omega-3s are

essential for brain function and may balance neurotransmitter activity, making emotional regulation easier.
- **Complex Carbohydrates.** Whole grains like quinoa, brown rice, and whole-wheat pasta can help regulate blood sugar levels, avoiding the spikes and crashes that can lead to irritability. They also stimulate the release of serotonin, often called the *"feel-good hormone."*
- **Protein-Rich Foods.** Lean proteins like chicken, turkey, and legumes can help keep your mind sharp and focused, reducing the likelihood of feeling overwhelmed by your emotions. These proteins contain amino acids that are precursors to neurotransmitters responsible for mood regulation.
- **Fruits and Vegetables.** Antioxidant-rich foods like berries, spinach, and bell peppers can combat oxidative stress linked to emotional instability and mood disorders. Their rich nutrient content can also supply the vitamins and minerals necessary for *optimal brain function*.
- **Probiotic Foods.** Emerging research suggests a strong connection between gut health and mood. Foods like yogurt, kefir, and fermented foods like kimchi and sauerkraut contain probiotics that may improve gut flora, which can impact your emotional well-being.
- **Water.** Though it seems simple, staying well-hydrated is necessary for cognitive function and mood regulation. Dehydration can lead to irritability and poor concentration, making managing emotions more challenging.

Besides that, here are tips for dietary success:

- **Meal Timing.** Regularly eating can help maintain steady blood sugar levels, reducing irritability and stress.
- **Moderation.** Extreme dietary restrictions can lead to nutrient deficiencies that negatively affect mood. A balanced diet is vital.

- **Plan and Prepare.** Planning meals can help you make healthier food choices, even when busy or stressed.

Paying attention to your dietary choices can equip your body with the nutrients it needs to manage emotional challenges like anger more effectively.

Lack of Personal Time

Parenting is a full-time job that rarely offers breaks, holidays, or personal time. The sheer relentlessness of the responsibilities can be exhausting. This is why the absence of this valuable *"me time"* can ignite feelings of anger.

- **Loss of Individual Identity.** Before becoming parents, people have established lives, interests, and activities that define them as individuals. The arrival of children shifts the focus, often making personal interests and pursuits secondary. Over time, this sidelining of personal identity can lead to resentment and unhappiness.
- **Lowered Coping Abilities.** Personal time is essential for emotional regulation and stress management. Activities like reading, exercising, or even taking a short walk serve as coping mechanisms for life's daily stressors. When these coping outlets are absent, parents might find that their ability to handle even minor irritations is compromised.
- **Accumulation of Tensions.** Minor irritations and frustrations can accumulate without personal time, like a pressure cooker gathering steam. Without the outlet of personal time to release some of this pent-up stress, the pressure can reach a boiling point, often released as an angry outburst.

- **Reduced Relationship Satisfaction.** Lack of personal time also impacts relationships. When parents are constantly *"on,"* they have less time with their partners, reducing communication and emotional connection. Feeling isolated or unsupported in a relationship can add another layer of emotional volatility.

Financial Stress

The constant worry about making ends meet, saving for emergencies, paying bills, or securing a child's educational future creates a strain that permeates multiple aspects of family life. Below are some ways financial stress can trigger anger in parents.

- **Heightened Emotional Sensitivity.** Emotional nerves are often frayed when under financial stress, leading to a heightened sense of sensitivity. Even small challenges or minor irritants can become disproportionately upsetting.
- **Reduced Patience.** Financial worries can consume mental energy, leaving less cognitive bandwidth for other issues, including parenting.
- **Feeling of Loss of Control.** A precarious financial situation can make parents feel like they are losing control over their lives. This perception can be highly stressful, and the instinctual human response to loss of control is often anger or aggression aimed at reclaiming authority or establishing boundaries.
- **Fear and Anxiety Manifesting as Anger.** Fear of being unable to provide for one's family is one of the most primal fears any parent can experience. When these anxieties become overwhelming, they can manifest as anger.

Exercise: Identifying Your Prime Triggers to Anger

The better you understand your triggers, the more equipped you will be to catch your anger early and address it. Follow this exercise to pinpoint your unique triggers.

Materials Needed

- Journal or piece of paper
- Pen

Instructions

1. **Reflect on Past Incidents.** Begin by thinking of three to five recent situations where you felt angry. Try to remember as many details as possible.
2. **Write Them Down.** On your piece of paper or in your journal, write down the following for each incident:
    - Where were you?
    - Who was involved?
    - What was said or done that triggered your anger?
    - What were you doing right before the incident?
    - How did you react?
3. **Look for Patterns.** After you have documented these incidents, read through your entries to see if there are any common elements.
    - Are certain people consistently involved?
    - Do particular types of situations trigger your anger?
    - Are there recurring themes or specific issues that make you angry?
4. **Categorize Triggers.** Try to sort these triggers into categories. Some common categories might include:
    - Financial stress
    - Parenting challenges

- Relationship issues
- Work stress
- Personal insecurities

5. **Rate Your Triggers.** On a scale from 1 to 10, rate how intensely each trigger affects your emotions. Doing so will help you identify which triggers to prioritize in your anger management journey.
6. **Reflect on Underlying Emotions.** For each trigger, jot down what emotions you feel besides anger. *Are you also feeling stressed, disrespected, insecure, or scared?* Sometimes, anger is a secondary emotion that masks your feelings.

After completing this exercise, you should have a clearer understanding of what triggers your anger. Keep this list accessible, and consider revisiting and updating it as you notice new or old triggers no longer affect you.

Chapter 3
Managing Your Emotions

Emotions can run high during parenting. The joy of a child's first steps, the frustration of a teenager's rebellion, the fear for their safety, the pride in their successes—*parenting is a rollercoaster of emotions.*

But what happens when these emotions start to take control? When does anger become a familiar visitor? This chapter is dedicated to helping you manage and understand your feelings, including self-awareness and various strategies to regain control.

Self-Awareness

Self-awareness is the conscious knowledge of one's character, thoughts, motives, and desires. Think of it like holding up a mirror to your inner self, understanding what you see, and using that knowledge to manage your emotional landscape. In the context of parenting, self-awareness becomes even more necessary. It is the first step toward managing your emotions and creating healthier relationships with your children.

Recognizing Your Emotions

Understanding and acknowledging what you feel is foundational to self-awareness. Instead of merely reacting to situations, you begin to observe and understand your emotional responses. This self-reflection enables you to say, *"Right now, I am feeling overwhelmed,"* or *"In this moment, I am beaming with pride for my child."*

Below are some tips for recognizing your emotions:

- **Tune into Your Body.** Beyond the whirlwind of daily tasks and responsibilities, take a moment to check in with yourself. *What sensations are present?* Maybe it is the heat of embarrassment on your cheeks or the tightness in your chest from stress.
- **Reflect on Your Thoughts.** Emotions and thoughts are intrinsically linked. *What is running through your mind? Are there recurring negative self-statements or concerns about your child that cue specific emotions?*
- **Assess Your Behavior.** Emotions often drive behavior. *Are you raising your voice, becoming withdrawn, or using sarcasm?* These actions can be telltale signs of underlying feelings.

After recognizing emotions, the next phase is to delve deeper. Pinpointing triggers and understanding the root causes of your emotions provide valuable insights. This awareness helps diffuse potentially explosive situations and fosters healthier coping strategies.

Understanding Your Emotional Patterns

Emotional patterns are habitual responses to situations and challenges, often formed over years or even decades. They can be positive, like expressing gratitude and love, or less productive, like resorting to anger or withdrawal when confronted with stress or conflict. These patterns are mental shortcuts your brain takes to deal with circumstances quickly, based on past experiences.

Recognizing your emotional patterns is the first step toward self-awareness. Self-awareness allows you to step back and examine your emotional responses objectively. *Are you quick to anger when your child disobeys? Do you retreat into silence when conflicts arise with your partner?*

Once emotional patterns are identified and decoded, you will gain the following:

- **Reflection over Reaction.** Recognizing emotional patterns allows parents to step back and reflect on their feelings before acting. This pause can mean the difference between a constructive response and a regrettable reaction.
- **Root Cause Analysis.** Understanding these patterns can help pinpoint the underlying causes or triggers. It might not just be a child's misbehavior causing anger; perhaps it is tied to an old personal experience or a deeper fear.
- **Empathy Boost.** Recognizing one's emotional patterns fosters empathy, as parents can more easily relate to their children's emotions. When you understand your emotions, you are better equipped to understand and validate your child's feelings.

Emotional Intelligence and Parenting

Emotional Intelligence (EI) is the ability to understand and manage your emotions and those of the people around you. It comprises a range of competencies, including emotional awareness, the ability to harness emotions to solve problems, and the capacity to manage emotions, which includes regulating one's own emotions and cheering up or calming down other people.

Below is how emotional intelligence fosters self-awareness.

- **Enhanced Emotional Vocabulary.** EI helps you better describe your feelings, not just as *"good"* or *"bad,"* but with specific terms like *"frustrated," "overwhelmed,"* or *"joyful."* Such an understanding can serve as an internal early warning system, helping you identify emotions before they escalate into more significant issues.

- **Improved Emotional Regulation.** Self-awareness allows you to manage your emotional reactions more effectively. You will find it easier to take a deep breath and count to ten before reacting to your child's latest escapade.
- **Mindfulness and Presence.** Emotional intelligence often goes hand in hand with being more present and mindful. When you are entirely *'at the moment,'* you are better positioned to pick up on your emotions and your child's, leading to more meaningful interactions.
- **Empathy.** As you become more aware of your own emotions, it becomes easier to recognize and understand the emotions of others—in this case, your child. This empathetic approach is vital for building a strong parent-child bond and helping resolve conflicts more compassionately.

Self-Regulation

Self-regulation is one of the most effective ways to manage your anger as a parent. This includes managing your emotions and reactions, even in challenging situations or triggers. Below are some strategies for self-regulation, from immediate techniques for calming down to long-term strategies for emotional management.

Techniques for Calming Down

In the heat of the moment, anger builds up, and it is necessary to have techniques that can help you calm down quickly, such as:

- **Deep breathing.** Take slow, deep breaths through your nose and out through your mouth. Focus on your breath and try to clear your mind of other thoughts.
- **Take a time-out.** If necessary, take a few minutes away from the situation. Go for a walk, listen to some calming music, or do something else that you find relaxing.

- **Talk to someone you trust.** Sometimes, talking about what makes you angry can help you calm down. Talk to a friend, family member, therapist, or counselor.
- **Practice relaxation techniques.** Many techniques, such as yoga, meditation, or progressive muscle relaxation, can help you calm down.
- **Visualize a calming scene.** Close your eyes and imagine a calming scene, such as a beach or a forest. Focus on the details of the scene and let your anger melt away.
- **Use positive self-talk.** Talk to yourself calmly and reassuringly. Tell yourself that you can handle the situation and do not need to get angry.

Mindfulness and Parenting

Mindfulness involves bringing one's full attention to the present moment non-judgmentally. It encourages observing thoughts, feelings, and sensations as they arise without trying to change or escape them.

Practicing mindfulness **helps parents become aware of their emotional state**, including triggers and early signs of anger. Instead of being caught off-guard by escalating emotions, parents can recognize the first flickers of irritation or frustration, allowing them the opportunity to take preemptive action.

Moreover, mindfulness **teaches parents to pause between stimulus and response.** When something upsetting happens—*like a child refusing to eat dinner*—a mindful pause can make the difference between yelling and addressing the situation calmly. This pause provides a buffer, allowing choice rather than an impulsive reaction.

Under mindfulness is objective assessment, which **encourages a detached observation of one's thoughts and feelings.** Parents can better assess whether their anger is proportionate to the situation or exacerbated by external factors like stress or fatigue. This objectivity can lead to more constructive solutions to conflicts.

To practical mindfulness, do the following:

- **Mindful Observation.** When feelings of anger arise, instead of reacting impulsively, try to observe your thoughts and feelings as if you were an outside observer. This can provide valuable insights into triggers and patterns.
- **Body Scan.** Sometimes, anger manifests physically—tense muscles, clenched fists, shallow breathing. Performing a quick body scan can help you recognize these physical cues and take steps to relax, such as loosening your grip or relaxing your shoulders.
- **Mindful Listening.** Often, conflicts with children arise from misunderstandings or feeling unheard. Listen to what your child is saying without immediately jumping to conclusions or formulating your response.

Long-Term Emotional Management Strategies

Unlike short-term strategies that may offer immediate relief in heated moments, long-term strategies equip you with the tools to recognize, understand, and manage your emotional responses over time. These strategies work at a foundational level, altering how you perceive and respond to potential triggers.

Long-term emotional management strategies include the following:

- **Cognitive Reframing.** Over time, parents can train their minds to reframe triggering situations. Instead of seeing a child's defiance as a personal challenge, it can be reframed as a developmental phase or an expression of individuality.

This shift in perception can reduce the intensity of the emotional reaction.
- **Self-care.** Consistently prioritizing self-care—*through regular exercise, adequate sleep, or engaging in hobbies*—ensures that parents are mentally and physically better equipped to handle stressors.
- **Continuous Learning.** Just as children grow and evolve, so do the challenges of parenting. Parents can adapt strategies and approaches by consistently updating their understanding of child development, communication techniques, and emotional intelligence.

Consistent use of long-term emotional management strategies promotes an innate ability to self-regulate.

Building Emotional Resilience

Adapting and bouncing back when things do not go as planned is called emotional resilience. Emotional resilience can help you, as a parent, manage your anger and respond to parenting challenges.

Developing Emotional Stamina

Like physical stamina, which allows you to sustain physical effort over an extended period, emotional stamina enables you to withstand and manage emotional distress, challenges, and setbacks without losing composure or effectiveness.

Having emotional stamina is necessary for anger management for the following reasons:

- **Reduced Reactivity.** Emotional stamina protects against knee-jerk reactions, enabling you to pause and assess the situation before responding. This can be particularly helpful in heated moments with your children, where an impulsive reaction might escalate the situation or impart the wrong lessons about emotional management.

- **Improved Decision-Making.** Emotional stamina allows you to think more clearly, even in emotionally charged situations. This clear-headedness can lead to better decision-making, which is essential when handling conflicts or disciplinary issues as a parent.
- **Greater Emotional Regulation.** Developing stamina helps identify your emotional triggers and understand your reaction patterns. This self-awareness makes it easier to control your responses and manage your anger more effectively.

To build your emotional stamina, do the following:

- **Emotional Skill-Building.** Learn techniques to de-escalate your emotions.
- **Healthy Coping Mechanisms.** Replace destructive behaviors, like yelling or slamming doors, with constructive outlets like exercise.
- **Seek Support and Guidance.** Talking to professionals like therapists or counselors who can provide expert techniques tailored to your emotional needs.

Building emotional stamina is a long-term commitment that requires consistent effort. The more you practice emotional control and effective coping, the stronger your emotional stamina will become.

Coping with Stress and Burnout

A heightened stress level can lead to a shorter emotional fuse, making anger more likely and intense. Hence, addressing underlying stressors and the potential for parental burnout is essential for anger management.

Physical exercise is not just good for your body; it also profoundly affects your mental health. Engaging in physical activity releases endorphins, which are natural mood lifters. They can also act as natural *'stress relievers,'* helping to dissipate the physical tension and arousal that often accompany anger.

Here are some exercise suggestions that you can easily incorporate into your routine to help manage anger:

- **Cardio Blast.** Cardio exercises release endorphins, quickly improve mood, and diffuse anger.
  1. Run in place or do jumping jacks for 30 seconds.
  2. Follow this up with high knees for another 30 seconds.
  3. Finish with a quick set of 10 burpees.
- **Box it Out.** The physical act of throwing punches can help you release pent-up aggression in a controlled environment.
  1. Stand in a boxing stance and throw a series of punches (jabs, hooks, uppercuts) into the air.
- **Quick Core Workout.** Engaging your core muscles requires focus and concentration, diverting your attention away from sources of anger.
  1. Do a series of planks, side planks, and Russian twists.
  2. Aim for 30 seconds for each exercise.
- **Stress Ball Slam.** Slamming something (safely) allows you to express your anger physically without causing harm or destruction.
  1. If you have a soft stress ball or even a soft toy, slam it onto a safe surface as hard as possible, then pick it up and repeat.
- **Mindful Walk.** Walking helps to clear your mind, and focusing on your breath can help lower stress hormones.
  1. Take a walk around your block or through a nearby park.

2. Focus on your steps and breathe deeply, matching your inhale and exhale with each step.

Moreover, parenting is demanding, and no one can do it perfectly. ***Accepting that imperfection is part of the process*** can relieve self-imposed stress. ***Setting boundaries***, like time for self-care, is essential. It is okay to say no or ask for help; doing so is a sign of strength and self-awareness, not weakness.

Regularly evaluating what is causing stress and how effectively you manage it can help you adjust your coping strategies.

Emotional Expression

Emotional expression refers to identifying, articulating, and effectively sharing feelings. When it comes to anger management, effective emotional expression allows one to process one's emotions, gain understanding from others, and build bridges instead of barriers.

Constructive Vs. Destructive Emotional Expression

Yelling, name-calling, or aggressively venting anger are ***destructive expressions*** that perpetuate a cycle of emotional escalation and tension within the family. These actions may provide a temporary release but often lead to regrets and long-term relational damage.

Meanwhile, ***constructive expression*** involves recognizing your anger and de-escalating the emotional state before communicating. Once calmer, you can articulate your concerns assertively but respectfully, aiming for resolution rather than conflict.

Components of Healthy Emotional Expression

Below are the components of a healthy emotional expression.

- **Clarity.** Instead of saying, *"You are making me mad!"* a more effective expression might be, *"I felt hurt when you disregarded my opinion."*
- **Assertiveness.** Involve standing up for one's rights while respecting others. It is not about being aggressive or passive; it is about stating feelings confidently without belittling or blaming.
- **Active Listening.** While expressing your emotions is crucial, so is listening. Active listening allows a fuller understanding of others' perspectives, reducing potential misunderstandings and conflicts.
- **Non-verbal Cues.** Remember, a significant portion of communication is non-verbal. Pay attention to body language, tone of voice, and facial expressions in yourself and others.

Tips for Constructive Emotional Expression

To effectively express your emotions, do the following:

- **Pause and Reflect.** Before reacting, take a moment to assess why you are angry and what specific action or words triggered this emotion.
- **Choose the Right Time and Place.** Waiting before discussing anger is sometimes better, especially if emotions run high. Also, ensure the setting is appropriate for an open conversation.
- **Use "I" Statements.** Frame the conversation regarding your own experiences and emotions without blaming or accusing. For example, say, *"I felt upset when this happened,"* rather than *"You make me angry when you do this."*

- **Be Solution-Oriented.** Focus on resolving the issue at hand rather than venting. Work together to find a solution that is acceptable for all parties involved.
- **Model Emotional Regulation.** Demonstrate effective regulation of your own emotions. Your ability to express feelings calmly and constructively can influence your child's emotional habits.

Journaling as Self-Therapy

Keeping a journal can be a powerful self-therapy tool for managing emotions like anger. Journaling offers the following benefits:

- **Immediate Emotional Release.** Writing down what you are feeling in the heat of the moment can diffuse the emotional intensity you are experiencing. This immediate act of writing can provide a form of emotional first aid.
- **Increased Self-Awareness.** Consistent journaling allows you to delve into the root causes of your anger, helping you understand its origins and the situations that often trigger it.
- **Problem-Solving.** A journal can serve as a space to brainstorm solutions constructively. Writing down potential solutions to a problem can be a far more effective strategy than stewing in your anger.
- **Tracking Progress.** Over time, the entries can serve as a record of your emotional journey. This longitudinal view can be uplifting when you notice that situations that once angered you no longer have the same effect.
- **Better Communication.** Writing down your thoughts helps you articulate them more clearly. This can be especially helpful when discussing your feelings with another person, allowing for a more constructive conversation.

Methods and Prompts for Effective Journaling

Some of the journaling methods you can do include the following:

- **Free Writing.** Write non-stop for a set time *(e.g., 10 minutes)* about what makes you angry, ignoring grammar and structure. The goal is emotional expression.
- **Graded Exposure.** Start by writing about minor irritations and gradually work up to more significant sources of anger.
- **The "ABCDE" Method.**
  - **A:** Describe the *activating event.*
  - **B:** Note your *beliefs* about this event.
  - **C:** Identify the *consequential emotion (in this case, anger).*
  - **D:** *Dispute* any irrational beliefs.
  - **E:** Note the new *emotion* you feel after this analysis.

The Role of Forgiveness

Forgiveness does not mean condoning or ignoring a wrongful act—yours or someone else's. Instead, it is about releasing the emotional burden of lingering resentment and anger. It is a conscious decision to let go of the need for retribution and to move on, thereby setting yourself free from an emotional prison.

Anger often creates a vicious cycle in a family dynamic. A parent's anger can induce stress or anger in children, which can, in turn, heighten the parent's emotional state. *Forgiveness acts as a circuit breaker.* By choosing to forgive, you take the first step in disrupting this destructive cycle, allowing for emotional recalibration and improved family relationships.

Unresolved anger can wreak havoc on your mental well-being and have physical consequences like increased blood pressure or stress hormone levels. *Forgiveness allows you to achieve internal peace*, contributing to emotional well-being, which can positively influence family life.

The Process of Forgiving

As parents, understanding and embracing the process of forgiveness can help manage your anger and teach your children constructive emotional habits. Here is how the process of forgiveness typically unfolds:

1. **Acknowledge the Anger.** Denying your feelings will only prolong your emotional distress and could lead to physical health problems.
2. **Understand the Source.** Once you have identified that you are angry, dig a little deeper to understand the source of your anger. *Is it a one-time occurrence or part of a pattern? Does it remind you of past experiences?* Understanding the roots of your anger helps you gain perspective, making it easier to address the actual issue rather than reacting to surface emotions.
3. **Express Your Emotions Constructively.** Communicate your feelings, but in a way that is constructive and conducive to resolution. This can be a conversation with someone who has angered you or a personal exercise like journaling. The aim is not to unload your feelings on another person but to articulate them in a way that promotes understanding.
4. **Make the Decision to Forgive.** Forgiveness is a choice that comes after understanding the situation and your feelings about it. *Decide to forgive as an act of self-care, not necessarily because the other person deserves forgiveness but because you deserve peace.* Remember, forgiveness is for your well-being; it allows you to let go of grudges, which are emotionally taxing to maintain.

5. **Take Constructive Action.** Sometimes, forgiveness involves setting new boundaries or changing certain behaviors to prevent future occurrences. In other cases, it might involve letting go of unrealistic expectations. Determine what changes are needed moving forward and be proactive in implementing them.
6. **Revisit and Reaffirm Your Decision.** Forgiveness is often not a one-time act but a process. You may need to revisit your decision to forgive, especially if old feelings of anger resurface. This is natural and does not mean you have failed in forgiving. It simply means you are human; forgiveness is a journey, not a destination.

Seeking Professional Help

Before seeking help, recognize and accept that there might be an issue. Some signs that you might benefit from professional help include:

- **Chronic Anger.** If you find yourself angry more often than not, or your anger lasts for extended periods and disrupts your daily life, this could be a sign that professional help is warranted.
- **Intensity.** When your anger seems disproportionate to the situation or excessively intense, it could indicate an underlying issue that might best be addressed with professional guidance.
- **Physical Manifestations.** Physical symptoms like chronic headaches, digestive issues, or even high blood pressure could indicate anger affects your health.
- **Impact on Relationships.** If your anger is causing tension or conflict within your family, affecting your relationship with your partner or children, this is a clear signal that professional input is needed.

- **Lack of Control.** If you have tried self-management techniques but can still not control your reactions, this lack of control might be better addressed in a structured setting with professional oversight.

Besides that, getting professional intervention can assist in the following:

Identifying Underlying Issues

Often, the triggers for anger are symptoms of underlying issues such as stress, anxiety, or past traumas. Professionals can help identify these root causes and provide targeted interventions for effective management.

Providing Tailored Strategies

Therapists, counselors, and psychologists are trained to offer evidence-based strategies for anger management. They can provide coping mechanisms tailored to your needs, which can be helpful if generic techniques have not worked.

Offering a Neutral Perspective

Talking to a professional offers a confidential, unbiased setting where you can openly discuss your feelings and frustrations. Their impartial viewpoint can provide new insights into your situation and behavioral patterns, which can be enlightening and liberating.

Enhancing Emotional Intelligence

Professional guidance can help you better manage your reactions to anger-inducing situations. With expert support, you can learn strategies to respond to triggers in a more controlled, thoughtful manner rather than reacting impulsively. A therapist can also assist you in pausing during heated moments to make more rational decisions before speaking or acting.

Long-Term Accountability

Regular check-ins with a professional provide accountability, making you more likely to adhere to your anger management strategies. It also allows for ongoing plan modification based on what is proving effective or ineffective.

Types of Professional Help Available

Below are the types of professional help you could get.

- **Counseling or Psychotherapy.** Individual or family sessions with a qualified therapist can help you get to the root causes of your anger and provide tailored coping strategies.
- **Group Therapy.** Sometimes, being part of a group grappling with similar issues can provide unique insights and support.
- **Psychiatry.** Medication may be prescribed to help manage underlying conditions contributing to your anger, such as anxiety or depression. However, medication is usually considered a last resort and is most effective when combined with therapy.
- **Anger Management Programs.** These structured programs offer a comprehensive approach to recognizing triggers, understanding emotional reactions, and learning coping mechanisms.

Whichever format you choose, do not hesitate to reach out if your anger is harming your children. You and your family deserve support.

Technology-Assisted Anger Management

Technology is not just for entertainment or work. It can also be a powerful tool for personal development. Regarding anger management, various technology-assisted solutions can complement traditional methods, making emotional regulation more accessible and often more immediate. Below are some ways technology can assist in managing anger effectively.

Apps for Mindfulness and Emotional Regulation

These are mobile applications designed to help users become more aware of their emotional states and provide techniques for self-regulation. Such apps may offer a range of features, such as guided meditation sessions, breathing exercises, and emotional tracking functionalities. They help by providing:

- **Instant Accessibility.** These apps are at your fingertips whenever needed, allowing immediate intervention when emotions escalate.
- **Customization.** Many apps offer personalization options, tailoring exercises, and tips to your specific needs and triggers.
- **Self-Monitoring.** Some apps have tracking capabilities to help you monitor emotional trends over time, providing insights into triggers and progress.
- **Family Involvement.** There are apps designed for parents and children, facilitating a family-centric approach to emotional regulation.

Virtual Counseling and Online Resources

Online counseling platforms connect you with certified therapists through video, chat, or voice calls. Similarly, various websites and online courses offer resourceful articles, worksheets, and video tutorials on anger management techniques.

Attending virtual counseling has various benefits, such as:

- **Convenience.** Virtual counseling eliminates travel, making it easier for busy parents to fit anger management into their schedules.
- **Anonymity.** The relative anonymity of online interactions can sometimes make it easier to open up about sensitive issues.
- **Cost-Effectiveness.** Online resources and virtual counseling can often be more affordable than in-person options.
- **Comprehensive Solutions.** Many online platforms offer multifaceted approaches to anger management, including one-on-one counseling sessions, group webinars, and self-help materials.

Integrating these technology-assisted methods into your anger management strategies makes the process more accessible and aligned with contemporary lifestyles.

Chapter 4
Communicating Effectively

This chapter delves into the essential aspects of effective communication with your child, recognizing its significance in parenting and anger management. Beyond just active listening, learn the various elements that contribute to successful communication within the parent-child dynamic, facilitating a deeper understanding and connection between you and your child.

Active Listening

Active listening is a way of interacting that needs the listener to fully concentrate, understand, respond, and remember what is being said. It is about being present and engaged in the conversation, showing empathy and understanding, and refraining from making judgments or giving unsolicited advice.

The Importance of Listening

Even though listening is an essential part of communication, it is often overlooked, especially in the parent-child dynamic. Perhaps you, as parents, usually focus on teaching, advising, or disciplining your children, forgetting that listening to them is equally necessary.

However, listening to your child shows them that you value their thoughts and feelings, which can boost their self-esteem and make them feel loved and understood. Knowing your child better can lead to more effective parenting tactics.

Active listening also helps in managing your anger. Listening carefully makes you less likely to react impulsively or let your anger take control. Instead, you are more likely to respond calmly and mindfully, which can prevent conflicts and strengthen your relationship with your child.

Techniques for Active Listening

Active listening involves more than just hearing the words your child says. It requires a conscious effort to understand their message and respond appropriately. Here are some techniques to help you become a more active listener:

- **Pay full attention.** Put away distractions and focus entirely on your child. Make eye contact and use body language to show you are engaged in the conversation.
- **Show empathy.** Try to understand your child's feelings and perspective. Show empathy through your words and actions, such as nodding or saying, *"I understand how you feel."*
- **Reflect and clarify.** Repeat what your child has said in your own words to ensure you have understood correctly. Ask clarifying questions if necessary.
- **Avoid interrupting.** Let your child finish speaking before you respond. Avoid jumping to conclusions or making assumptions.

Listening to Understand, Not to Respond

A common mistake in active listening is focusing on how to react rather than trying to understand what the other person is saying.

When you listen to respond, you often miss the nuances of what is being said, and your focus is on constructing your rebuttal or defense, which prevents you from understanding the other person's viewpoint.

On the other hand, listening to understand brings a different dynamic into the conversation. You become more empathetic and open to the other person's feelings and thoughts, even if you disagree with them. It defuses tension and facilitates more constructive discussions.

Imagine a situation where your teenager comes home past curfew, and you are angered and worried.

Listening to Respond

Teen: *"I am sorry, I lost time while studying at Sarah's house."*

Parent: *"Studying? You know the rules, and you broke them. You are grounded for the next week!"*

Here, the parent needs to focus on understanding why the teenager is late but on asserting authority and setting punitive measures.

Listening to Understand

Teen: *"I am sorry, I lost time while studying at Sarah's house."*

Parent: *"I was distraught. Can you help me understand how you lost track of time?"*

Teen: *"We had a major test to prepare for, and I turned off my phone so it would not be a distraction."*

Parent: *"Thank you for letting me know. I understand it is important, but keeping time is also important. Let's discuss how you can balance both next time."*

In the second scenario, the parent tries to understand the child's perspective. As a result, the conversation opens up a pathway for a constructive solution rather than leading to escalated conflict.

This does not mean there would not be consequences, but it does mean that they can be reached through understanding and dialogue rather than anger and unilateral decisions.

Conflict Resolution

Despite best efforts, disagreements and conflicts will inevitably arise in parent-child relationships. However, avoiding or suppressing conflict is not the solution. These clashes present opportunities to guide your child through conflict in a constructive manner. Successfully navigating these disputes helps teach vital skills like communication, emotional regulation, and compromise—abilities that will serve children well later in life.

So, how can you guide your child through conflict in a positive way? Here are some critical steps:

- Identifying the underlying cause of the anger.
- Actively listening to the child's perspective.
- Expressing the parent's feelings in a non-confrontational manner.
- Collaboratively seeking solutions.

To understand the process, suppose a teenager named Alex comes home past curfew, and his mother, Lisa, is furious. Instead of an explosive confrontation, here is how conflict resolution could play out:

1. **Calm Down Before Conversing.** Lisa recognized her heightened emotions and decided not to approach Alex immediately. She takes a few minutes to breathe deeply and calm down.
2. **Open the Conversation Constructively.** Instead of accusingly asking, *"Why are you late again?!"* Lisa says, *"I was

worried when you did not come home on time. Can we talk about what happened?"
3. **Actively Listen.** Lisa allowed Alex to explain that he lost track of time helping a friend with homework and that his phone battery died, so he could not inform her.
4. **Express Feelings Calmly.** Lisa responded, *"I understand things can come up. When you are late, I get scared that something might have happened to you. Please keep the curfew or inform me if you are running late."*
5. **Collaborate on Solutions.** They discuss potential solutions together. Perhaps Alex can set an alarm as a reminder, or they can invest in a portable charger for his phone.
6. **Reaffirm the Relationship.** Lisa ended the conversation by expressing that her concern came from a place of love, and Alex acknowledged that he would be more mindful of time and keep her informed.

Using conflict resolution in this manner, Lisa and Alex resolved the immediate issue, strengthened their relationship, enhanced their communication, and set the stage for handling future disagreements.

Building a Peaceful Home Environment

Having a peaceful home environment means conflicts are less likely to occur and more likely to be resolved successfully. In building one, here are some tips:

- **Establish Clear, Fair Rules.** Having clear, fair rules can reduce conflicts over expectations and limits. Involve your child in creating these rules to improve their understanding and compliance.
- **Foster Open Communication.** Encourage your child to share their feelings, needs, and concerns. Regular family meetings can provide a safe space for this dialogue.

- **Prioritize Quality Time.** Spending quality time together can improve your relationship with your child, making conflicts less likely and easier to resolve.

Using effective conflict resolution techniques and building a peaceful home environment, you can turn disputes into opportunities for growth and learning. This can lead to a healthier, more harmonious relationship with your child and a more peaceful, less angry home atmosphere.

Non-Verbal Communication

Communication goes beyond the limits of spoken or written words. Much of our communication is non-verbal, covering elements such as body language, facial expressions, gestures, tone of voice, and volume. Non-verbal communication often conveys more than words; understanding can enhance your interactions with your children.

Body Language

Body language includes facial expressions, body postures, gestures, eye contact, and physical distance *(proxemics)*. It can describe a broad spectrum of emotions and attitudes, often more accurately than words.

For example, crossed arms may indicate your child feels defensive, while relaxed shoulders suggest openness. Lack of eye contact can signal avoidance or shame. Noticing these cues provides insight into your child's inner world.

Likewise, your body language as a parent matters too. An aggressive stance while disciplining could escalate tension, but an open, compassionate presence might defuse conflict. Children are highly attuned to nonverbal signals, and your body language impacts them deeply.

Below are common body languages and their meaning.

- **Nodding.** It often indicates agreement, understanding, or encouragement for the speaker to continue.
- **Tapping Feet or Fidgeting.** It may suggest impatience, nervousness, or restlessness.
- **Prolonged Eye Contact.** It can be interpreted as interest, dominance, or challenge. However, in some cultures, it might be considered rude or aggressive.
- **Avoiding Eye Contact.** It could be seen as evasiveness, discomfort, or lack of confidence.
- **Touching the Nose or Mouth.** Sometimes, it indicates doubt, uncertainty, or lying. However, do not rely on this cue alone to judge someone's honesty.
- **Leaning In.** Suggests interest and attentiveness to the speaker or topic.
- **Mirroring.** This is when one person unconsciously adopts another's body language. It often indicates rapport and alignment in thoughts or feelings.

Tone and Volume

Tone and volume are crucial elements of non-verbal communication. The same words can convey different meanings based on how they are said. A calm, gentle tone can convey warmth and understanding, while a harsh, loud tone can communicate anger and hostility.

Awareness of your tone and volume as a parent is vital, especially when angry or upset. A harsh tone or high volume can escalate disputes and make your child feel threatened or defensive. Conversely, a calm, steady tone can de-escalate confrontations and make your child feel safe and understood.

The Power of Positive Reinforcement

Positive reinforcement is based on the idea that behaviors followed by pleasant consequences are more likely to be repeated. In the context of parenting, this means rewarding your child's acceptable behaviors to encourage them to continue those behaviors.

A reward or reinforcement can take many forms. It could be vocal praise, a hug, a special privilege, or a small treat. However, it should be something your child values, and it should be given quickly after the desired behavior.

For instance, if your child shares a toy with a sibling without being asked, you might give them a warm smile and say, *"Sharing your toy was good. That was very kind of you."* This immediate, positive response encourages your child to repeat the behavior in the future.

Techniques for Positive Reinforcement

There are many ways to implement positive reinforcement in your parenting. Here are a few techniques:

- **Immediate Feedback.** Reinforce the behavior as soon as possible. The sooner you acknowledge good behavior, the more likely it will be repeated.
- **Be Specific.** Instead of general acknowledgment like *"Nice work,"* be specific about what you recognize. Say something like, *"I noticed you put your toys away neatly!"* Specificity helps the child understand precisely what they did well.
- **Use Verbal and Non-Verbal Rewards.** Verbal praise is effective but can be supplemented with non-verbal

rewards like claps, hugs, or high-fives. Occasionally, small tangible rewards like stickers or a favorite treat can be effective.
- **Be Consistent.** If you acknowledge a behavior once and ignore it the next time, the child may become confused about what is expected.
- **Involve children in the Reward Process.** Let the child have a say in what the rewards are. This will make them more invested in the process.
- **Frequency Over Magnitude.** Small, frequent rewards are often more effective than larger, infrequent ones. The point is to make positive behavior a habit; frequent reinforcement is usually more effective for habit formation.
- **Avoid Reinforcing Undesired Behavior.** It's essential to be mindful of how specific actions may encourage behaviors you wish to diminish. For instance, if a child receives extra screen time as a response to crying or throwing a tantrum, they may learn to repeat that behavior to gain similar rewards. Instead, focus on positively reinforcing behaviors you want to encourage.
- **Scale Rewards Appropriately.** As the desired behavior becomes a habit, consider scaling back the rewards and moving to a more intermittent reinforcement schedule. This helps the child transition from external motivations to internal ones.

Instilling Boundaries

Boundaries in the parent-child relationship define acceptable behavior and what is not. Boundaries can be physical, such as not entering your child's room without knocking, or mental, such as not making derogatory comments about each other.

Understanding boundaries involves recognizing that each person has different needs and rights. For instance, your child has the right to their thoughts and feelings, while you, as a parent, should work to earn their respect through understanding, empathy, and consistent, fair treatment. These boundaries help maintain a healthy relationship balance, ensuring neither party feels disrespected nor exploited.

Setting and Enforcing Boundaries

Creating boundaries is a process that includes clear communication, consistency, and follow-through. Here is how you can approach it:

1. **Identify the Need.** Start by identifying the behaviors that need to be handled. *Is it about respecting privacy or how you talk to each other?*
2. **Communicate Clearly.** Once you have found the need, communicate it clearly to your child. Be explicit about what is okay and what is not.
3. **Be Consistent.** Consistency is key when it comes to limits. If a boundary is not regularly upheld, it can confuse and undermine its purpose.
4. **Follow Through.** If a boundary is crossed, follow through with the agreed-upon result. This reinforces the boundary's value.
5. **Review and Adjust.** As your child grows, your boundaries may need to change. Check and adjust regularly as needed.

Boundaries and Respect

Boundaries are not just about rules; they are about respect. By setting limits, you teach your child to respect your needs and rights, and this lesson often extends to their interactions with others.

In addition, when you respect your child's limits, you show them that their needs and rights are essential, too. This mutual respect can lead to a healthier and more balanced friendship.

Setting clear boundaries helps avoid situations that might trigger your anger. For example, if you have a boundary about not being interrupted during certain times, this can reduce instances of annoyance and anger.

As you continue your journey in effective parenting, remember the value of boundaries. They are not just rules set in stone but are dynamic lines of respect that can help create a healthier and more harmonious parent-child relationship.

Exercise: "The Mirror Technique"

This exercise aims to enhance listening skills, increase empathy, and foster transparent, effective communication between parents and their children.

Materials

- Pen and paper for each participant

Instructions

1. **Set the Stage.** Gather in a quiet space where you and your child can sit facing each other. Let the child know that this is a special time to talk and listen so that they can better understand each other.
2. **Establish Ground Rules.** Make it clear that the aim is to listen to each other without interrupting. No judgments or immediate solutions—just listening.
3. **Topic Selection.** Either you or your child can choose a topic for discussion. The topic should be something both parties have opinions on but may not fully understand each other's perspective. For example, *"The importance of chores"* or *"Weekend activities."*

4. **Parent Speaks First.** Speak first; express your views, feelings, and thoughts for about five minutes. Your child should listen attentively without interrupting.
5. **Child Mirrors.** After you finish speaking, your child will *"mirror"* what they have heard. This means summarizing what you have said without adding personal opinions. For example, *"I hear you saying that chores are important because they teach responsibility."*
6. **Parent's Confirmation.** Confirm whether your child's summary is accurate or provide clarification.
7. **Switch Roles.** Now, your child speaks about their views on the topic while you listen without interrupting.
8. **Parent Mirrors.** Like Step 5, you will summarize your child's words. Again, the aim is to understand, not to judge or offer solutions.
9. **Child's Confirmation.** Your child confirms or clarifies your summary.
10. **Write it Down.** Both you and your child, take a moment to write down what you have learned from this exercise about your and the other's viewpoints.
11. **Reflect and Share.** Both share what you have written and reflect on the experience. Discuss any new insights gained and how communication can be improved.
12. **End with Gratitude.** Close the exercise by expressing gratitude for each other's time and insights.

After the exercise, consider discussing the following:

- Was it easy or difficult to listen without interrupting?
- How did it feel to be listened to attentively?
- What did you learn about your and each other's feelings and viewpoints?

This exercise can be repeated with different topics and is designed to help parents and children learn to communicate more clearly and empathetically with one another.

Chapter 5
Improving Parent-Child Relationships

Spending one-on-one time with each child is essential for parents seeking to manage anger effectively. This dedicated time together builds a more profound understanding and stronger emotional bonds between parents and children. As a result, children feel more secure, and parents are less prone to irritation, reducing potential anger outbursts.

Building Quality Time

Giving each child separate, focused attention without distractions helps you avoid daily frustrations that can accumulate and lead to anger flare-ups. This bonding time makes children feel listened to, valued, and secure.

Designating Regular One-on-One Time

Set aside at least 15 minutes daily for one-on-one time with each child. Consistency and follow-through are necessary—treat this time window as unassailable in your schedule.

Determine the optimal time of day when you can be fully mentally present. Morning rituals before the daily rush allow you to start the day positively. Evening wind-down routines pave the way for restful sleep. You can also schedule it during periods already built into your day, like commuting time.

For children who thrive on regularity, ***keep the timeframe the same daily.*** For others, build flexibility, ***maintain consistency***, and only cancel in emergencies. Follow-through demonstrates that despite your many responsibilities, your relationship remains number one. This loyalty provides security for children amidst the turbulence of daily life.

Take a different approach for pre-teens and teenagers who tend to value privacy. Rather than insisting on the designated time, explain that you miss spending time together and would like to rebuild your connection. Start gradually with brief check-ins and mutual activities to reestablish rapport. ***Earn more access to their world by demonstrating non-judgmental listening.***

Single parents with multiple children can ask friends or relatives to babysit others one-on-one. You can also trade childcare with other parents to support each other. Building a support network is essential.

When you cannot get help, ***find creative ways to spend time with each child on weekends.*** Set up independent activities for the others, like reading or crafts. For infants or high-needs children, look for moments during caregiving to connect, like talking while rocking them or singing during diaper changes.

For families with infants or high-needs children requiring more physical care, ***adjust your expectations for one-on-one time.*** Look for opportunities for connection during caregiving tasks. Chat while rocking them to sleep or sing songs while changing diapers. Schedule focused activities like reading or playing with toddlers when they are most alert and engaged.

Build one-on-one time into family outings and vacations as well. Take walks together, enjoy mini-golf or museum visits in pairs, or spend an afternoon focused on one child's favorite activity. Protect this exclusive time even when schedules are more fluid.

Special time provides space to discover your child's unique interests. Follow their lead in conversations and activities to gain insight into their inner world. Develop mutual interests into shared passions that provide natural relationship bonds.

Learning Child's Interests

Using your dedicated one-on-one time to uncover each child's unique interests and passions can provide valuable insights that strengthen your bond and help avoid anger triggers.

Start by ***observing their independent play.*** Instead of seeing it as a way to pass the time, feel the stories they create. The characters, scenes, and roles they act out can give clues about what captures their imagination. To understand them better, ask open-ended questions about the deeper meaning behind their play.

Focus on the creative process rather than judging the result when you find them deeply engrossed in art or craft activities. If your child is deeply into their project, gently ask what inspired their choice of colors, textures, or images. Art can provide a glimpse into their inner world, so avoid putting your interpretations on it.

Explore the topics that fascinate them, whether it is dinosaurs, dance moves, or types of mushrooms. Children's interests often differ from what adults expect. Taking the time to explore their diverse passions allows you to see life from their point of view. Instead of changing the subject, match their enthusiasm.

Encourage them to explore potential interests, even if they seem fleeting. For example, if a child watches chicks hatching in a science class with intense attention, it might indicate a growing fascination with birds or biology. Even tiny sparks of curiosity should be gently explored, not treated like an interrogation.

Pay attention to the books, movies, and music they love. Favorite stories can express a child's values and sensibilities. Music playlists might reveal influences from friends and their experiments with self-identity. Scenes in movies that make them laugh or cry provide insight into their emotional connections.

Keep an eye out for talents or skills that surpass your expectations, like a knack for technology, a nurturing way with animals, or keen insights into people. Knowing your child's authentic self without preconceived notions often brings pleasant surprises. Appreciate their uniqueness.

Remember that independence includes the freedom to make mistakes. Allow your child space to discover what resonates with them and what does not, trusting their guidance. Interests can change over time, so use your judgment to decide when to guide them gently and when to let them explore on their own.

Maintain a balance between actively engaging with their interests and listening carefully. Do not expect a one-sided conversation or rapid-fire questions. Let the conversation unfold naturally, then summarize what you have heard without making judgments. Encourage discussion rather than giving lectures.

One-on-one time is the key to understanding your child's inner world—their dreams, values, perspectives, and emotions. By taking a genuine interest in who they are and what they love, you can build deeper connections and create shared experiences that strengthen your relationship and head off anger triggers before they start.

Removing Distractions

Children are sensitive to divided attention. Even subtle distractions can signal that you are not engaged in the moment, reducing the quality of your time together and causing frustration.

Before your designated time, **be proactive about managing technology.** Turn off televisions, silence your phone, and put devices away out of sight. Refrain from responding to messages or taking calls unless there is an emergency. If work demands availability, notify colleagues you will be offline during this time. **Select activities that require face-to-face interaction,** like board games or art projects. Passive entertainment, like watching movies together, does not equate to quality emotional engagement.

Make your child the priority by **training your mind to immerse in the moment.** When you notice your focus slipping, gently bring it back. If interruptions occur, calmly explain why you must briefly divert your attention, keeping apologies or frustration to a minimum. Refocus on the particular time as soon as possible. When breaks happen frequently, reconsider when you have designated time.

Get your child involved in safeguarding quality times, too. Explain the importance of having their parent's complete focus and ask for their suggestions to make it distraction-free. When children recognize distractions as mutual *"enemies,"* it prevents them from feeling responsible. Use visual signals like wearing a unique bracelet, hat, or other tactile reminders that you are in your exclusive time bubble.

Inform extended family or friends not to drop by unannounced during treasured one-on-one time. Being *"unavailable"* during this time protects your schedule. **Designate a consistent spot just for your special time,** whether at a park, a reading nook, or a local coffee shop. A consistent setting removes environmental distractions and provides a tangible reminder of the significance of this parent-child time.

Protecting your dedicated time together demonstrates its status as a non-negotiable priority. Purposefully engineer your schedule and surroundings to eliminate distractions rather than allowing it to fall victim to daily diversions. Your unwavering presence conveys unconditional acceptance and understanding that strengthen your bond.

Fostering Open Communication

When tensions inevitably arise, quality communication paves the pathway to cooperative conflict resolution versus anger escalation.

Regular Family Meetings

Setting aside time for regular family meetings provides a forum for open dialogue in an intentional rather than reactive way. These discussions allow grievances to be aired, joys and concerns shared, and household rules and boundaries reinforced.

Keep meetings brief; sessions over 20 to 30 minutes often need more focus, especially with young children. ***Schedule at consistent intervals,*** weekly or monthly, when energy levels are optimal. Rotating facilitation roles gives everyone a chance to take leadership.

Collaboratively develop an agenda of topics to cover so discussions remain organized. Solicit input from all family members—make meetings participatory. ***Establish rules*** for listening respectfully and not interrupting others.

Ensure the environment feels relaxed and casual, perhaps gathering on the living room floor with snacks. Lighthearted rituals like singing a particular song can initiate meetings on a unifying note. ***Start and end with appreciation*** to further cultivate a positive atmosphere.

Vary activities to maintain engagement. Have each person take turns responding to a question of the day, play interactive games, or create an art project together. Keep a family journal of highlights from each gathering.

Regular family forums foster openness, allowing members to be heard, feel involved in decisions, and strengthen understanding. This prevents frustrations from being surprised, only to erupt later.

Nonviolent Communication Model

Nonviolent communication provides a constructive approach to expressing perspectives and needs calmly, which can help defuse anger.

It involves four components:

- **Observation.** Describing a situation factually, free of judgment. Rather than saying, *"You made a mess,"* you, as a parent, would observe, *"There are toys scattered on the floor of the living room."*
- **Feelings.** Express emotions arising from the observation. *"I feel tired and overwhelmed."* Identifying and owning your feelings prevents misdirecting frustration onto others.
- **Needs.** Share underlying needs tied to those feelings. *"I need order and rest."* Revealing your authentic needs prevents projecting them onto others.

- **Request.** Make a specific request to address unmet needs. *"Would you please help me clean up the toys so I can relax before making dinner?"* This provides a constructive path forward.

Such a compassionate communication approach opens the door to discovering mutual solutions. Children learn emotional awareness and conflict resolution skills. Anger gives way to cooperation, strengthening family ties.

Resolving Conflict Constructively

Unresolved parent anger can damage family relationships and child well-being. However, managing emotions during conflicts is challenging. With practice, you can learn and model constructive conflict resolution, teaching children invaluable anger-coping skills.

Identifying Root Causes

In the heat of an argument, it is easy to react hastily without understanding what truly underlies the dispute. Taking time to unpack the root causes of conflicts will help you seek to manage anger constructively.

Step Back and Calm Down

When tensions run high, intense emotions can cloud your perspective. Step back to calm your anger before trying to analyze the situation.

Take a few deep breaths and clear your mind. Go for a short walk to get fresh air and decompress. Try a simple meditation or mindfulness activity to achieve a relaxed state. The goal is to create internal stillness to examine the conflict calmly and objectively.

Approaching disputes from a place of relaxation rather than agitation allows you to understand better causes instead of reflexively reacting in anger. With cooler heads, resolution becomes more feasible.

Talk It Out

Have an open discussion where each person describes their view of the conflict without interruption. Listen attentively, overcoming the urge to form counterarguments while they speak. The goal is to gain a clear picture of all perspectives.

Ask clarifying questions to fill in the blanks rather than making assumptions. Often, underlying misunderstandings exacerbate surface conflicts. Seek to comprehend rather than convince.

Dig Beneath the Surface

Explore beneath-surface issues to uncover core needs. A child refusing to help with household chores may seem openly defiant. However, the discussion may reveal attention cravings or unclear expectations are at play.

Empathetically explore the feelings behind your child's actions. *Are they acting out due to anger, insecurity, or rebellion? What unspoken needs might their behavior represent?* Making your best effort to grasp their inner world diffuses conflict.

Analyze your role as well. *Did you make incorrect assumptions about motives? Did you allow external stressors to impact your mood and reactions negatively?* Taking ownership of your contributions can also help defuse your child's anger.

Get Support If Needed

When stuck analyzing the conflict's origins, engage a third party. A counselor, friend, or grandparent may identify factors neither of you can see clearly. They may also be able to mediate, helping you both feel understood.

Commit to Investing Time

In many parent-child disputes, scratching beneath the surface reveals interconnected issues and misunderstandings. Unraveling the roots of conflicts requires dedication, patience, and emotional restraint.

Avoid seeking quick fixes or unilateral pronouncements of fault. Be willing to invest significant time and respectfully unpack all facets. The upfront effort pays off by diverting anger into collaboration.

When you remain calm, listen, and search for root causes, disputes become teachable moments rather than sources of lingering resentment. Though not always comfortable, helping your child see beneath surface conflicts provides an invaluable life lesson in emotional intelligence. With time and guidance, they gain the tools to self-reflect rather than react when angered.

Finding Mutual Understanding

After identifying the underlying sources of a conflict, try to ***understand each other.*** Put aside your anger and try to find things you and your child agree on. Doing so will help you work together to solve the problem in a kind and caring way.

When getting into arguments, you often consider it a battle you must win. There is a need to show that you are right. But thinking this way usually makes things worse and hurts relationships. Instead, ***look at the disagreement with an open mind,*** like being willing to listen instead of fighting. This way, you can understand what your children are thinking, what they want, and what they are trying to do. Rather than being opponents, you become partners trying to find a solution that works for both of you.

Also, show an interest in what your child is saying. Listen without interrupting or showing that you do not care. Do not roll your eyes or act like you are uninterested. After they talk, ask questions to make sure you understand what they mean.

You might want the same things underneath the things you are arguing about. Both of you want to find a solution that keeps your respect and trust for each other. Talk about these things you have in common to make the argument less like a fight and more like a team effort.

Once you know what is meaningful to both of you, ***try to come up with ideas that meet your needs.*** For example, if you are fighting about chores, discuss how to share the work somewhat based on what each person can do.

Compromising and Apologizing

Seizing the roots of a conflict and airing mutual perspectives leads to resolution through compromise and apology. Taking ownership showcases emotional maturity, which is essential for anger management.

In solution discussions, ***keep an open mindset.*** Integrate parts of your child's suggestions and avoid turning disagreements into power struggles.

Articulate your reasoning but allow for adjustments. Phrases like *"I am open to making changes"* or *"Let me know your concerns with this approach"* foster collaboration.

Besides that, **unrealistic proposals should be guided with understanding.** For instance, *"I see your point, but there is a safety issue. What if we try another way?"* This promotes compromise without escalating anger.

When you have directly contributed to a disagreement, **apologize sincerely.** Statements like *"I am sorry for my words"* or *"I regret raising my voice"* highlight responsibility. Apologizing sets an example for children, showing them that admitting mistakes during disputes signifies strength.

After resolving the issue, **reaffirm your bond.** Address any residual tension and express the desire for constructive conflict handling in the future. Honor agreements from the resolution to show your commitment to cooperative solutions.

Mastering compromise and apology equips children with vital relationship skills, especially when emotions flare. Over time, maintaining emotional composure and mutual respect can defuse intense disagreements.

Chapter 6
Enhancing Adaptability

Children undergo rapid development changes. You must adapt to adjust your parenting appropriately to prevent rigid approaches that could cause conflicts. This chapter outlines techniques to help you adapt expectations, boundaries, and ineffective strategies to meet your children's evolving needs. It also covers monitoring personal triggers.

Adjusting to Changing Needs

You must adapt flexibly as children grow to avoid anger over unmet expectations and forced milestones.

Accommodating Child's Development

Child development is not a linear path but a series of progressions and regressions. It encompasses physical, emotional, cognitive, and social changes a child undergoes as they grow. These milestones show typical development and can offer insights into a child's world at each stage.

- **Infancy (0 to 2 years).** At this stage, children are rapidly growing and dependent on their caregivers. Milestones include *physical activities* like crawling and walking, emotional attachments, and early speech sounds. As a parent, you might feel overwhelmed due to sleep deprivation and the constant needs of the baby.

- **Early Childhood (3 to 6 years).** When children become more independent, they start exploring their surroundings with curiosity. Key milestones include *language development, basic problem-solving skills,* and *forming relationships outside the family.* Challenges in this stage are setting boundaries and managing tantrums.
- **Middle Childhood (7 to 11 years).** Here, children start to form a sense of self and understand their place in the broader world. They develop more sophisticated cognitive skills, develop essential peer relationships, and seek autonomy. Often, you will grapple with balancing freedom and setting limits at this stage.
- **Adolescence (12 to 18 years).** This is a period of identity exploration. Teenagers develop abstract thinking, become more aware of societal norms, and often test boundaries. For you, managing their budding independence while ensuring safety can be challenging.

Renegotiating Boundaries

Your child's needs and abilities change as they grow, so their rules and responsibilities should also be updated. What is suitable for them at one age might not be ideal as they age.

Let the children have more freedom, as they show they can make good decisions and act more grown-up. They should get a chance to make their own choices. Do this gradually and ensure they are responsible for their actions to prevent anger caused by unclear rules.

When they get upset, consider whether the balance between freedom and limits suits their age. A child who acts without thinking needs more rules and supervision. A responsible teenager, meanwhile, can have more freedom, like staying out later or having more social time. Adapting helps prevent bad feelings.

Involve your children in making new rules. Make it something you work on together. When everyone understands and agrees on the rules, it is easier to cooperate and avoid arguments. They can help create rules that make sense for their age and what they can do. When everyone is on the same page, it helps everyone get along better and grow emotionally.

Modifying Approaches

To manage anger, be ready to change how you do things as your child grows, even if it means giving up on methods you have used for a long time.

Do not let your pride or ego get in the way when you see your actions are not working or causing too many arguments. For instance, being strict with punishments might have worked when your child was younger, but it can lead to rebellion when they become teenagers. In such cases, it is better to switch to problem-solving together.

Being adaptable shows you respect your child's uniqueness instead of trying to make them fit a specific mold. As your child grows, look at what helps them develop and what does not without getting angry about it.

This flexibility prevents you from getting stuck in rigid ways of thinking that can lead to anger when your child's path does not match your vision.

Monitoring Personal Triggers

Managing anger requires paying close attention to the situations and circumstances that ignite your emotions, such as:

Identifying High-Risk Situations

Identifying situations that provoke anger or frustration is vital. Common triggers include specific times, locations, or stress-inducing activities. Recognizing these allows you to strategize your response.

Some of the high-risk situations for parents include the following:

- **Morning Rush.** When everyone transitions from sleep, the early hours of the day can be chaotic. Ensuring kids are dressed, fed, and equipped for school or other activities within a tight timeframe can strain patience, especially when children are slow to respond or easily distracted.
- **Meal Times.** These are opportunities for family bonding, but disagreements over food preferences can lead to tension. Whether a child refuses vegetables, demands specific foods, or does not value the effort put into meal preparation, such moments can trigger frustration.
- **Bedtime Battles.** Ideally, bedtime is a peaceful winding-down period. Kids may negotiate for one more story, get out of bed numerous times, or become thirsty or hungry. The repeated delays can wear thin on a parent seeking some downtime.
- **Homework Help.** Assisting with homework requires patience, especially with challenging subjects. Children's resistance, lack of interest, and procrastination can make this a tension-filled experience.

- **Public Outbursts.** Nothing is as challenging as a child's tantrum in a public setting. Managing the child's behavior while conscious of public judgment can be stressful.
- **Sibling Rivalry.** Continuous bickering or physical altercations between siblings demand intervention. Such conflicts can be emotionally draining as parents strive to mediate without seeming to favor one child over another.
- **Non-cooperation.** An outright refusal to help with chores or flouting house rules can lead to power struggles, testing parental authority and patience.
- **Teen Rebellion.** The teenage years bring unique challenges. Late nights, pushing boundaries, and defiant actions can cause worry, frustration, and anger for parents trying to protect and guide their growing children.
- **School-related Stress.** Negative feedback during parent-teacher meetings or learning about one's child being bullied can evoke strong emotions, leading to feelings of protectiveness, disappointment, or anger.
- **Playdates and Social Interactions.** Playdates offer social growth for kids, but differences in upbringing or behavior can lead to conflicts. Additionally, leaving kids unsupervised at friends' homes may stir anxiety.
- **Technology Battles.** The digital age brings arguments about screen time duration, appropriate content, and digital interactions. Setting and maintaining boundaries can become a recurrent flashpoint.
- **Health and Safety Concerns.** Seeing your child take risks or resist necessary treatments can spike anxiety and anger. This is particularly heightened when the child's well-being is perceived to be at stake.
- **Misbehavior in front of Guests.** When children choose the moment visitors arrive to misbehave, it can be particularly embarrassing, leading parents to feel judged or disrespected.

- **Back-talk and Disrespect.** Sudden verbal challenges or inappropriate responses can catch parents off-guard, testing their ability to respond calmly and assertively.
- **Special Events Stress.** High expectations around holidays or birthdays can lead to disappointment if children behave unpredictably or are unappreciative. While meant to be joyous, these events can have undercurrents of tension.

Awareness of these situations and having strategies in place to approach your child can help navigate the complexities of parenting.

Recognizing Warning Signs of Anger

To manage your anger effectively, observe yourself and recognize the signs that show you are getting angry as soon as possible, such as:

- **Physical Signals**
    - *Clenched fists or jaw.* You might notice that when you are beginning to get irritated, your hands ball into fists, or your jaw tightens almost instinctively.
    - *Tension in shoulders or neck.* Stress often manifests physically, particularly in the neck and shoulders. You might feel a stiffness or tightness creeping in.
    - *Rapid heartbeat or breathing.* As anger escalates, you may find your heart racing or your breathing becoming more shallow and fast.
    - *Feeling hot or sweaty.* Suddenly, there is a heat wave, or you might sweat unexpectedly.
- **Emotional Indicators**
    - *Irritability or short temper.* The most minor things might start to annoy you, even if they usually would not.

- *Feeling overwhelmed or anxious.* A sense of dread or inability to cope with even minor challenges might dominate.
- *Increasing frustration over small matters.* Everyday inconveniences become sources of significant frustration.
- *Sudden mood swings.* You might find yourself jumping from calm to furious in a short period.

- **Cognitive Signs**
  - *Constantly thinking about what upset you.* Despite other distractions, your mind keeps returning to the source of your irritation.
  - *Imagining confrontational scenarios.* You might catch yourself daydreaming about arguments or confrontations that have not happened.
  - *Blaming others for personal feelings.* Instead of recognizing internal sources of anger, you place the blame squarely on others.
  - *Catastrophizing or expecting the worst in situations.* When thinking about future scenarios, you only envision adverse outcomes.

- **Behavioral Cues**
  - *Raising the voice or shouting.* You might start speaking louder without realizing it, even when unnecessary.
  - *Slamming doors or objects.* Physical expressions of anger, such as hitting things, become more frequent.
  - *Sudden withdrawal from conversations or situations.* Instead of confronting issues, you might start avoiding them altogether.
  - *Engaging in aggressive driving or behaviors.* Actions become more impulsive, and you might take more risks than usual.

- **Changes in Routine**
  - *Difficulty sleeping or frequent nightmares.* Even when you try to rest, your mind might remain active,

replaying stressful events or concocting worrisome scenarios.
- *Increased use of alcohol, drugs, or other coping mechanisms.* You might find solace in substances or behaviors that offer a temporary escape.
- *Avoidance of social interactions or events.* Instead of seeking company, you prefer to be alone to avoid potential triggers.
- *Overeating or loss of appetite.* Your eating patterns become irregular, either consuming too much or too little.

- **Communication Patterns**
  - *Speaking in a sarcastic tone.* Your words carry a sharper edge, even if you are unaware.
  - *Interrupting or not listening to others.* Patience in conversations dwindles, and you find yourself talking over people.
  - *Using aggressive or passive-aggressive language.* Your choice of words might become more hostile, even if veiled in sarcasm or indifference.
  - *Criticizing or belittling others.* Instead of constructive feedback, your comments turn more negative.

- **Interactions with Children**
  - *Impatience with minor mistakes.* The small missteps of your children, which once seemed inconsequential, now elicit strong reactions.
  - *Reacting disproportionately to children's behaviors.* A minor act of defiance might invoke a much stronger reaction than it should.
  - *Withdrawing affection or giving the silent treatment.* Instead of addressing issues, you might withhold affection or avoid your child.
  - *General intolerance or lack of understanding toward a child's needs.* Your ability to empathize or understand your child's perspective diminishes.

Eliminating or Minimizing Triggers

Once you figure out what makes you angry, actively work to cut or lessen those things in your daily life. While you cannot always wholly avoid every trigger, you can take steps to make them bother you less often and less intensely, such as:

- **Morning Routines**
    - *Waking up earlier.* Setting the alarm a few minutes earlier ensures you have ample time before attending to your children. This *"me-time"* can be used for meditation, a quiet coffee, or mentally preparing for the day.
    - *Preparing the night before.* Laying out clothes, packing lunches, and organizing breakfast items the night before can drastically reduce morning stress. When things are pre-planned, there is less room for last-minute chaos.
- **Crowded Places**
    - *Shopping during off-peak hours.* This avoids the stress of navigating a crowded store and often means faster check-out times and better inventory selection.
    - *Choosing quieter venues.* For social outings, consider quieter, less crowded places. This could mean a local park instead of a busy amusement park or a quaint cafe over a bustling restaurant.
- **Family Interactions**
    - *Setting clear expectations.* Discuss the expected behavior Before activities like chores or homework. This way, children understand what is required, reducing potential conflicts.
    - *Consistent routines.* Predictable routines provide children with a sense of security and reduce the chance of resistance or tantrums.

- **Handling Defiance or Misbehavior**
  - *Using a calm voice.* Addressing misbehavior calmly often results in better cooperation from the child. It also models the behavior you want your children to adopt.
  - *Taking a "time-out."* Before reacting impulsively to misbehavior, parents can take a short break to calm down, ensuring a more measured response.
- **Avoiding Overwhelm**
  - *Prioritizing tasks.* Instead of feeling overwhelmed by a long to-do list, prioritize tasks, focusing on the most pressing issues first.
  - *Delegate.* Delegating tasks can alleviate personal stress, whether to older siblings, a partner, or even hired help.

With persistent effort, you can identify and address your anger triggers to either get rid of them or make them less problematic. No one expects you to put up with a constant stream of annoyances. As you regain control over the things you can change, you also restore control over your emotions. This allows you to show how to manage anger instead of being a victim of uncontrolled anger. Personal growth creates a more peaceful, cooperative, and connected family environment.

Maintaining Perspective

At times, frustration can overwhelm you, causing you to lose sight of the bigger picture and react hastily in the heat of the moment. To stay emotionally grounded during these moments, consider a few key strategies:

Tracking Progress Over Time

Effectively managing anger is a gradual process that requires a long-term approach. While daily irritations can test your patience, keeping track of your progress over weeks and months helps you see the bigger picture. Journaling can be a helpful tool for documenting your journey in anger management. It allows you to acknowledge your achievements and gain perspective, especially during challenging times.

Allocate five minutes each evening to **record your day's highlights and low points,** thoughtfully reflecting on each event. Note situations that triggered your anger and describe how you responded, highlighting what worked and what did not.

Be specific about the techniques you used to calm yourself and any helpful support. Share instances where you successfully resolved conflicts through deep breathing or taking a break to cool down. These positive examples can boost your motivation when you face setbacks.

Document further emotional breakthroughs, such as recognizing your irritation early or considering your child's perspective before reacting. These signs of emotional growth often go unnoticed in your daily life. Your anger journal helps you celebrate both minor and significant achievements.

Review your past entries regularly to identify any recurring patterns. *What consistently triggers your anger, and do specific times of day challenge you more? How has your response to similar situations changed over time? Are your mood swings becoming less frequent?* Monitoring your journey provides tangible evidence of your progress.

Share insights and milestones from your journal with your loved ones. Your partner can help you identify areas where you've improved or offer an external perspective. Discussing your achievements creates accountability and reinforces your commitment to managing anger. It also sets an example for your child, demonstrating the self-awareness needed for anger management.

In addition to your journal, ***use mental reminders to gauge your progress***. In the morning, anticipate potentially frustrating situations, such as driving to a sporting event. Acknowledge any anxiety, but visualize yourself staying calm, even in traffic jams. Later, reflect on how you managed your anger during the actual situation. These regular mental check-ins contribute to self-awareness.

For more quantitative data, ***rate your daily anger on a scale of 1 to 10 in the evening***. Take note of any factors that seem to influence your scores, like the quality of your sleep, your level of physical activity, or your child's behavior. Some apps are available to track your emotional states and identify triggering events. These objective patterns can provide valuable insights.

Maintaining perspective means focusing on the overall direction rather than individual days. Like the stock market, daily fluctuations are normal, but the long-term trend indicates progress. Celebrate your successes and learn from your setbacks without allowing them to define you. A challenging day with anger outbursts doesn't erase the weeks of diligent effort you've put in.

Continue to keep your mindset focused on the bigger picture. *Are your episodes of anger becoming less frequent and less intense overall? Are you regaining your composure more quickly? Are you getting better at identifying your triggers?* Approach setbacks and slips with self-compassion, viewing them as opportunities for ongoing growth and learning.

Then, renew your commitment to long-term change. Maintaining perspective will propel you forward on your journey to master anger and improve your family relationships.

Focusing on Positive Intent

When children act in ways that make parents angry, thinking positively can help parents respond with understanding instead of making things worse with accusations and assumptions. This means giving your child the benefit of the doubt and trying to find the good reasons behind their behavior. Shifting your focus to positive intentions turns anger into opportunities for growth and talking.

Consider a child who responds with sarcasm. Initial reactions might be that they are being defiant or trying to challenge you. But digging deeper might reveal they are emulating peers or expressing discomfort about something unrelated. Addressing the behavior is essential, but doing so without condemning the child is critical. A gentle approach, such as, *"Speaking like that can hurt feelings. Let us discuss this respectfully,"* can be effective.

Besides that, when a child neglects their chores or responsibilities, it might not always be defiance. Perhaps they forgot or were preoccupied. For recurring issues, like consistent incomplete homework, understanding the root cause, such as difficulty grasping the subject, can be beneficial.

Managing anger also requires introspection. When mistakes occur, focusing on self-improvement rather than self-blame is necessary. There will be instances when firmness is needed, but coupling it with understanding can foster a healthier dialogue.

Arguments, while challenging, are also opportunities. Highlighting shared objectives and framing problems as collaborative challenges can defuse tension. If a child reacts strongly, understanding that their response might stem from feeling unheard or overwhelmed can help guide the conversation toward resolution.

Positivity is infectious. Assuring a child of their worth, even in times of error, reinforces their self-worth. Internally, combating pessimistic thoughts with more benevolent interpretations can reshape one's perspective, strengthening trust and reducing hostility.

Chapter 7
Professional Help and Skills Building

To make your efforts to manage anger more effective, you can get help from professionals. These experts, like therapists and counselors, have much knowledge and use proven methods to help you.

Seeking Therapeutic Help

While you can learn some anger management skills independently, talking to a therapist has benefits. Therapists know a lot about how the mind works and how people behave. They can determine what makes you angry and why you think the way you do. With their help, you can understand your thoughts better and learn to express your feelings well.

In therapy, they focus on different things to help you manage your anger better:

- **Cognitive-behavioral Therapy (CBT).** About changing unhelpful thoughts and behaviors that make you angry. You do exercises to learn practical skills.
- **Mindfulness Practices.** Therapists teach you mindfulness and meditation techniques to become more aware of your emotions and control your anger when it happens.
- **Communication Skills.** Therapy often helps improve how your family talks to each other. Learn to listen better, express yourself constructively, and solve conflicts.

- **Child Development.** Therapists teach you about how children grow and develop. This helps you understand why your child might do certain things that make you angry. It enables you to have more reasonable expectations.
- **Finding the Real Causes.** Therapists also help you figure out what's making you angry. It could be past traumas, problems in your relationships, mental health issues, or substance use. By dealing with these root causes, you can manage your emotions better.

Different Types of Anger Management Therapy

Anger management therapy comes in various forms to suit different needs:

Individual Therapy

Engaging in individual therapy provides a unique and personalized experience tailored to your specific anger triggers and reactions. Here, you work closely with a therapist in a confidential setting, delving deep into personal histories, underlying emotions, and experiences that may be contributing to your anger. The therapist helps you recognize these triggers, develop coping strategies, and establish healthier behavioral patterns. This therapy's private nature often allows for candid discussions about personal issues that you might not feel comfortable sharing in a group setting.

Group Therapy

Group therapy creates a community of individuals facing similar challenges, providing a space to share experiences, frustrations, and successes. Facilitated by a trained therapist, these sessions offer a platform for mutual support and encouragement. Participants can learn from one another, understanding that they are not alone.

Listening to varied experiences allows participants to see their issues from different angles and helps them know diverse coping mechanisms. Witnessing others' progress and sharing in their victories can be therapeutic.

Family Therapy

Family dynamics can contribute to or exacerbate anger issues. Family therapy sessions involve the entire family or relevant members. The goal is to improve communication, address familial triggers, and build a more supportive environment. Involving everyone ensures that all members understand each other's perspectives, challenges, and needs. The therapist aids in mediating discussions, setting boundaries, and fostering understanding, aiming to reduce conflict and strengthen familial bonds.

Online Therapy

With technological advancements, therapy has expanded beyond traditional face-to-face sessions. Online therapy offers flexibility, making it easier for those with tight schedules or geographical limitations to access help. Via video conferencing, individuals can engage with therapists from their homes. Some platforms also provide supplementary resources, such as reading materials, interactive lessons, or chat options, to enhance the therapeutic experience. This mode of therapy can be especially beneficial for those who might be hesitant to attend in person due to stigmas or personal reservations.

Finding the Right Fit

Choosing the right therapy tailored to your needs can make a difference in navigating parenting challenges. Below is a deeper look into finding the appropriate anger management therapy:

- **Consider the Therapist's Expertise.** Work with therapists who specialize in anger management and have experience with parental challenges. Their insights can be more relevant and actionable.
- **Check Accessibility and Flexibility**
  - *In-person vs. online sessions.* While in-person sessions can be more personal, online options offer convenience, especially for busy parents.
  - *Frequency.* Depending on the severity of the anger issues and availability, decide whether weekly, bi-weekly, or monthly sessions are suitable.
- **Ask About Techniques and Tools.** A competent therapist will employ evidence-backed techniques. They also provide resources or exercises for parents to practice at home, reinforcing therapy sessions.
- **Seek Recommendations.** Personal recommendations can be invaluable. Friends or family members who have undergone similar therapy can provide insights. Additionally, professionals like pediatricians or school counselors might have credible references.
- **Evaluate Affordability.** While therapy's benefits can be life-changing, find options within your budget. Some therapists might offer flexible payment options, ensuring that finances do not hinder access to quality care.
- **Gauge Personal Comfort.** The success of therapy often hinges on the comfort and trust between the therapist and the patient. Feeling understood and safe is essential for open communication and progress.
- **Assess Progress Over Time.** Reflect on whether the therapy is making a tangible difference in anger management. Communicating openly with the therapist about progress and any necessary modifications is vital.
- **Explore Group Workshops or Classes.** Dedicated anger management courses, especially those designed for parents, can be a valuable supplementary resource. They

often provide practical tools and strategies in a structured format.
- **Stay Updated.** The field of therapy is continually evolving. Staying informed about new techniques or methods can introduce fresh perspectives or tools for better anger management.
- **Prioritize Self-Care Outside of Therapy.** Beyond formal therapy, integrating self-care practices like regular exercise, hobbies, adequate sleep, and a balanced diet can mitigate stress and anger.

While seeking anger management therapy, be proactive, informed, and patient. Everyone's journey is unique, and what works best will vary from person to person.

Benefits of Counseling and Therapy

The unique benefits of one-on-one or family therapy for anger management include:

- **Clinical Perspective.** Therapists provide an impartial professional viewpoint on dysfunctional behaviors based on clinical experience supporting many families. Their observations enlighten blind spots.
- **Customized Treatment.** Anger management therapy is tailored to your unique situation, challenges, and goals. Therapists get to know you to determine optimal therapeutic techniques.
- **Coping Skills.** Equipped with a toolbox of clinically proven anger management strategies, including emotional awareness, communication tactics, self-care, and more.
- **Insight Development.** Therapy fosters greater self-awareness about anger triggers, physiological responses, thought patterns, and behavioral cycles, precipitating positive change.

- **Supportive Accountability.** Ongoing therapy provides accountability for sticking with your anger management goals. Checking in with a therapist reinforces commitment.
- **Healthy Modeling.** Demonstrating your commitment to anger management therapy models constructive behavior. It teaches children how to improve themselves proactively through outside help.
- **Family Strengthening.** Family therapy heals relationships damaged by chronic parental anger and models healthy dynamics. It provides a forum for restoring trust and communication.

Seeking counseling demonstrates courageous dedication to personal development. An outside expert's support accelerates your progress in managing anger for more peaceful family relationships.

Anger Management Classes

Anger management classes are structured so parents can learn effective strategies for handling anger in a supportive group setting. These classes are led by experienced professionals who provide expert guidance and help you practice proven techniques for managing your anger.

Evidence-Based Techniques

Certified anger management classes use strategies proven to work through scientific research. These strategies can help parents improve their anger management:

- **Cognitive Restructuring.** A process of challenging and altering maladaptive, often irrational thought patterns that amplify emotional reactions. Participants in anger management classes are introduced to this technique to help them discern when their cognitive patterns are

intensifying their anger disproportionately. Through a step-by-step method, you are guided to replace these heightened thoughts with ones that are more balanced and rooted in reality. This helps provide a realistic perspective on events, reducing the chances of explosive reactions.
- **Cathartic Release.** While many individuals suppress their emotions, cathartic release promotes expressing these feelings in a controlled manner. In a secure and structured environment, you might be encouraged to shout, cry, or even physically vent *(like punching a pillow)*. This therapeutic approach is grounded in the belief that holding intense emotions can be harmful. The controlled release offers temporary relief from these feelings, ensuring you do not accumulate and cause more significant outbursts in the future.
- **Problem-Solving Training.** Anger can often result from frustrations stemming from unresolved problems. This training focuses on enhancing your problem-solving capabilities. This approach bolsters your self-efficacy by helping you delineate problems, brainstorm potential solutions, evaluate these solutions without letting overpowering emotions cloud judgment, and devise actionable plans. Feeling more competent in addressing issues often diminishes the intensity of anger experienced.
- **Relaxation Skills.** Anger causes physiological responses—increased heart rate, tensed muscles, and rapid breathing. Relaxation techniques, therefore, are taught to counteract these reactions. By mastering skills such as deep breathing exercises, progressive muscle relaxation, and even mindfulness exercises, you can quickly deploy these techniques in real-life anger-inducing situations, curbing the intensity of your reactions.
- **Emotional Intelligence.** Self-awareness is a crucial component of emotional intelligence—recognizing your

emotions as they arise. Enhancing emotional intelligence involves honing this awareness, understanding the triggers behind anger, mastering control over emotional responses, and fostering empathy. You practice recognizing and moderating your reactions through interactive exercises like role-playing, leading to more constructive responses in real-world situations.

- **Communication Tactics.** Misunderstandings and poor communication can exacerbate feelings of anger. Anger management classes often emphasize the importance of healthy communication skills. This encompasses actively listening to others, expressing yourself assertively without resorting to aggression, and strategies to de-escalate conflicts. Engaging in guided practice sessions with other participants aids in refining these skills.
- **Exposure Therapy.** Facing your triggers can reduce the intensity of the reaction over time. In a safe environment, you might be presented with simulations of scenarios that typically elicit anger *(e.g., a child's disobedience)*. Repeatedly being exposed to these situations under guidance helps gradually reduce the intensity of the emotional response and equips you with strategies to handle such instances more effectively.
- **Self-Exploration.** Understanding the causes of your anger is pivotal. Some individuals might find their anger rooted in past traumatic events, underlying mental health challenges, or a lack of effective coping mechanisms. Through reflective activities like journaling or group discussions, you delve into these underlying issues. Unpacking and confronting these roots can be therapeutic and instrumental in shaping healthier responses to triggers.

Peer Support

In anger management classes, both experts and peers offer support. The solidarity from peers experiencing similar challenges is invaluable. Recognizing you are not the only one facing parental anger is reassuring and reduces the weight of handling this emotion solo. Sharing experiences highlights that occasional anger does not label you a *"bad"* parent. Stories from parents, both compassionate and occasionally angered, serve as inspirations.

Open discussions allow self-reflection and encourage self-forgiveness. Hearing about others' mistakes reinforces the understanding that no parent is flawless. This environment promotes sharing rather than concealing challenging experiences. The collective drive to evolve is motivational. Witnessing peers' determination in the face of setbacks instills belief in sustainable change.

Peers offer emotional reinforcement as a support system to prevent discouragement, especially during challenging times. They commend minor accomplishments, motivating continued effort. The group dynamic also fosters responsibility. The upcoming class can remind you to practice newly acquired techniques, ensuring consistency in your efforts.

Under expert guidance, class discussions remain solution-driven and devoid of unconstructive critique. The setting is designed to be safe and conducive to growth. Peers double as practice partners, providing invaluable feedback. Role-playing scenarios demonstrate the practical application of techniques. Feedback illuminates strengths and areas of potential refinement.

Interactions with peers can unveil unrecognized patterns in your behavior, enhancing self-awareness. When others pinpoint improvements you might overlook, it elevates your confidence.

Connections made in these sessions often extend beyond the classroom, solidifying lasting friendships. This community shows that you are part of a bigger whole and fosters mutual support and healing.

Specialized Curriculum

A specialized curriculum tailored for parents dealing with anger offers a structured pathway to understanding and regulating anger, ensuring a healthier family environment. Such a curriculum recognizes that the strains of parenthood—balancing work, childcare, and personal life—can sometimes escalate emotions, potentially leading to unwanted outbursts or prolonged resentment.

A few critical aspects of this curriculum include:

- **Holistic Approach.** Unlike generic anger management courses, this curriculum is specifically designed for parents. It considers the myriad situations you encounter, from toddler tantrums to teenage rebellion, offering strategies that directly apply to these contexts.
- **Self-awareness Modules.** The curriculum encourages you to delve deep into your emotional triggers, allowing you to recognize and understand your anger's roots. This self-awareness forms the foundation for effective anger management.
- **Skill Building.** Through interactive sessions and practical exercises, you learn to diffuse explosive situations, communicate more effectively, and employ relaxation techniques. Role-playing, for instance, helps you practice calm responses in various scenarios.
- **Child-Centric Perspective.** The curriculum emphasizes the impact of parental anger on children's emotional and psychological development. Understanding the potential

harm of unchecked anger can motivate you to regulate your emotions more.
- **Resource Availability.** Provided with various tools, including journals, digital apps, and reading materials, to support their journey outside the classroom. These resources help reinforce lessons and offer ongoing support.
- **Peer Support.** Group sessions allow you to share your experiences, challenges, and successes. This community aspect can motivate and support individuals throughout their anger management journey.

Communication Skill Building

Mastering communication abilities provides invaluable tools for managing parental anger. Nonviolent communication, conflict resolution tactics, and conveying empathy transform family interactions and relationships. Evidence-based approaches equip parents to defuse rather than fuel conflicts.

Nonviolent Communication

Nonviolent communication is a helpful way for parents to express their thoughts and needs calmly. This approach can defuse anger and solve family problems through understanding and compassion.

Created by psychologist Marshall Rosenberg, nonviolent communication has four steps:

- **Observe.** Describe situations without using judgmental labels that might make others angry. Instead of saying, *"Your room is a mess!"* you can observe, *"There are clothes and toys on the bedroom floor."*
- **Express Feelings.** Share your emotions calmly using *"I"* statements instead of directing frustration at others. For

example, say, *"I feel overwhelmed and stressed when I see this mess,"* to express your feelings.
- **Identify Needs.** Recognize the underlying needs that drive your feelings. *"I need order and organization to feel calm"* communicates a genuine need without projecting it onto others in anger.
- **Make Requests.** Make explicit, constructive requests to address unmet needs and emotions. Saying, *"Could you please put away your clothes and toys to help create order?"* invites cooperation.

This four-step approach helps you understand your child's emotions and needs before reacting angrily. It also teaches children skills like self-awareness, empathy, and conflict resolution by example.

Benefits of Nonviolent Communication for Parents

Nonviolent communication offers several advantages for parents dealing with anger:

- **Defuses Conflict.** Expressing feelings and needs calmly helps reduce tension and avoids blame, criticism, and demands that often lead to family conflicts. Constructive requests bypass unproductive arguments.
- **Teaches Self-Awareness.** Identifying your feelings and needs builds self-awareness and emotional intelligence. It enables you to express your experiences without assuming that your children are intentionally causing frustration, leading to better anger management.
- **Models Skills for Children.** When parents communicate nonviolently, children learn to recognize emotions, express themselves constructively, and resolve disagreements through dialogue instead of anger. These skills promote emotional maturity.

- **Promotes Collaboration.** Instead of demanding compliance, making requests encourages children to work together to solve problems. Nonviolent communication shows respect and seeks cooperation, strengthening family bonds.
- **Focuses on Solutions.** Nonviolent communication emphasizes finding constructive solutions to unmet needs, shifting the focus from past grievances to resolving underlying issues. This helps move beyond anger and work on root problems.
- **Promotes Empathy.** Sharing feelings and needs without judgment fosters empathy. When family members understand each other's perspectives, it encourages compassion.

Getting Started with Nonviolent Communication

To make nonviolent communication a habit, practice is necessary. Here are some tips to begin applying its principles:

- **Observe.** Describe situations objectively without using labels that can trigger anger. For example, instead of blaming your child for making a mess, say, *"The living room is messy."*
- **Breathe.** When you feel anger rising, take a few deep breaths before responding. This gives you space to connect with your feelings and needs.
- **Use "I" Statements.** Express your feelings and needs using *"I"* language, like *"I feel..."* and *"I need..."* instead of blaming *"you."* Take ownership of your experience.
- **Identify Specific Needs.** Get comfortable articulating specific needs, like respect, consideration, order, autonomy, or understanding. Avoid making these demands.
- **Make Small Requests:** Phrase your requests as small, positive actions, such as *"Please put your toys away,"* rather

than making enormous, vague demands. Small steps are more likely to invite cooperation.
- **Practice Reflective Listening.** When you receive conflicting messages, reflect on what you heard without judgment before crafting your response. Seek to understand before responding.

With practice, nonviolent communication can transform anger into opportunities for growth. It offers a compassionate approach to resolving family conflicts cooperatively and respectfully.

Conflict Resolution

Parental anger can escalate when conflicts are not addressed effectively. With the right approach to conflict resolution, disagreements can transform into personal development opportunities and avoid prolonged bitterness.

At the onset of a disagreement, *initiate a dialogue that clearly outlines the issue*, steering clear of blame or accusations. Involved parties to empathize with each other's perspectives, avoiding entrenchment in their standpoints.

Often, the apparent reasons for disagreements obscure underlying shared objectives. For instance, while you and your children might argue about the specifics of spending time together, both might inherently desire more quality time as a family. Recognizing these mutual goals can create a sense of unity.

Engage in collaborative problem-solving, suggesting solutions that cater to everyone's needs and sidestepping dominance battles. While deliberating over possible solutions, remember that arriving at a middle ground may be more beneficial.

Should emotions intensify, momentarily ***stepping away from the discussion*** can be beneficial. When returning to the conversation, prioritize mutual agreement over securing a personal victory in the debate.

After reaching a consensus, recap the agreement terms to ensure clarity and consistency. Acknowledging and apologizing can mend strained relationships if any mishaps occur during the discussion.

Navigating disagreements constructively, familial harmony is maintained, and relationships are fortified.

Chapter 8
Rebuilding Trust After an Outburst

The trust is the foundation of the parent-child relationship, underpinning both parties' emotional and psychological well-being. Outbursts, particularly when frequent or unpredictable, can erode this delicate bond, leaving lasting impressions and challenging the very essence of this trust. Recognizing the impact of such outbursts is vital to nurturing and maintaining a healthy relationship between parent and child.

Consequences of Not Rebuilding Trust

Trust, the invisible glue that holds relationships together, often becomes taken for granted. In the context of a parent-child dynamic, its presence or absence can shape the course of that relationship. When trust is damaged and left unrepaired, the aftermath can ripple through the immediate relationship and the broader aspects of the child's life, such as:

Erosion of Relationship Foundation

When trust wanes, so does the stability of this foundational bond.

Trust is an essential ingredient for fostering emotional intimacy. As trust erodes, the emotional connection between parent and child can become strained. This distance might manifest as reduced affection, a lack of open conversations, or hesitation in turning to each other during times of need.

A relationship steeped in trust encourages learning and guidance. A child might resist advice without trust, seeing it as interference rather than well-intended counsel. Parents, in turn, may feel sidelined, unsure of their role or efficacy in their child's life.

Developmental Impact on the Child

A lack of trust alters the parent-child dynamic and can have profound developmental implications for the child. For instance—

- **Emotional Repercussions.** A sustained lack of trust can breed insecurity and vulnerability in children. They may constantly grapple with the fear of judgment or ridicule, inhibiting their natural tendencies to explore and express.
- **Psychological Strains.** Beyond immediate emotional upheavals, long-term distrust can shape a child's psyche. This might manifest in issues such as anxiety disorders, chronic self-doubt, or tendencies towards isolation.
- **Social Implications.** Children model their social interactions based on foundational relationships, like those with parents. A mistrustful parent-child dynamic can make them wary of other relationships, potentially stunting their social skills and challenging interpersonal connections.

Increased Misunderstandings

Trust acts as a translator in many ways. When present, it can help clarify intentions, emotions, and actions, allowing for more accurate interpretations of behaviors. In its absence, however, every action can be misread, and every word misconstrued, leading to the following:

Skewed Perceptions

The absence of trust has a way of warping the interpretations of the actions and words of others, such as:

- **Distorted Reality.** Without trust, the clear lens through which one might view actions and intentions gets clouded. A child's simple request or a parent's advice can be seen as manipulative or controlling, distorting the reality of situations.
- **Projected Fears.** Without trust, underlying fears and insecurities can dominate perceptions. These fears often project onto benign interactions, making them seem more threatening than they genuinely are.
- **Heightened Sensitivity.** When trust is eroded, there is a heightened sensitivity to potential slights or insults. Even an innocent comment can be misconstrued, leading to overreactions or unnecessary hurt.

Conflict Escalation

The bridge of understanding, built on trust, becomes shaky when that trust is damaged. This instability can turn minor differences into significant confrontations:

- **Low Threshold for Disagreements.** In a scenario where trust is compromised, patience wears thin. It takes less to trigger a disagreement, and resolutions become harder.
- **Lack of Benefit of Doubt.** Trust allows for giving the benefit of the doubt in uncertain situations. Without it, every ambiguity can be interpreted negatively, leading to assumptions that amplify conflicts.
- **Defensive Stances.** When trust is lacking, parents and children might approach interactions with a defensive posture. This defensiveness can lead to the premature escalation of disputes as each party braces for conflict.

Feedback Loops

Mistrust can initiate a vicious cycle, where one instance of mistrust breeds more instances, making the restoration of trust increasingly tricky:

- **Reinforcement of Mistrust.** Every misunderstanding stemming from a lack of trust reinforces the belief that the other person is untrustworthy, further deepening mistrust.
- **Avoidance Patterns.** Over time, to avoid confrontations, either party might start evading genuine interactions, leading to even more distance and a lack of understanding.
- **Emotional Residue.** Past misunderstandings or conflicts can leave an emotional residue if not addressed. This baggage influences future interactions, making it easier to fall back into patterns of mistrust.

Diminished Emotional Safety

When trust between a parent and child erodes, it profoundly affects their sense of emotional safety and well-being. Here are some nuances of this consequence:

Seeking External Validation

When children feel emotionally unsafe within the family unit, they may turn to external sources for validation and acceptance, leading to:

- **Peer Pressure Susceptibility.** Children might become more susceptible to peer pressure, believing that conforming to external expectations will gain them the validation they crave.

- **Over-reliance on Digital Connections.** In the digital age, children might turn to social media or online platforms for affirmation, which can sometimes expose them to unhealthy environments or cyberbullying.
- **Risk-taking Behaviors.** Seeking external validation can lead some children to engage in risky behaviors, believing that these actions might earn them a place of acceptance or popularity among peers.

Decreased Personal Growth

A lack of emotional safety can stifle personal development in children:

- **Avoidance of New Experiences.** Children might become wary of new experiences or challenges, fearing failure or additional sources of conflict.
- **Impaired Problem-solving Skills.** Due to the lack of open communication and fear of conflicts, children might not develop the necessary skills to address and resolve their challenges.
- **Stunted Emotional Resilience.** Children might not develop the emotional resilience required to navigate life's ups and downs, leading to struggles in adulthood.

Building Emotional Walls

To protect themselves, children might construct emotional barriers affecting their interpersonal relationships:

- **Difficulty Trusting Others.** The trust issues originating from the parent-child relationship might extend to other relationships, making it hard for children to trust friends, partners, or even their judgment.

- **Fear of Vulnerability.** Children might associate vulnerability with potential hurt, leading them to guard their emotions and never truly open up, even in safe spaces.
- **Reluctance in Seeking Help.** Stemming from fear of judgment or further conflicts, children might avoid seeking help even when they genuinely need it, whether emotional, academic, or personal.

Techniques to Rebuild Trust

Once broken, trust is not easy to mend. But with consistent effort, understanding, and patience, damaged trust after an outburst can be rebuilt, leading to a healthier and more harmonious relationship.

Open Dialogue

Assumptions, silence, or misunderstandings can compromise trust. Cultivating a culture of open communication between you and your children can set the foundation for trust regeneration:

- **Expressing Vulnerabilities.** Sharing your fears, insecurities, and concerns allows more profound insight into behavior and motives. This level of honesty can dissipate built-up barriers.
- **Feedback without Blame.** Constructive criticism, delivered without an accusatory tone, facilitates trust-building dialogues and avoids defensive reactions.
- **Creating a Safe Space.** Establishing a non-judgmental environment where you and your child feel safe expressing your feelings can foster trust.

Consistent Behavior

While words carry weight, actions echo louder in the realm of trust:

- **Follow Through.** Keeping your word, especially in promises or commitments, acts as a foundation for reinforcing trust.
- **Setting and Respecting Boundaries.** Clear boundaries affirm mutual respect, promoting an environment where trust can flourish when set and respected.
- **Transparency in Actions.** Clarifying the motivations or reasons behind actions eliminates ambiguity, ensuring your child does not feel sidelined or neglected.
- **Predictability.** Establishing routines or patterns in behavior can ease anxieties, further solidifying trust.

Apologize Sincerely

A genuine acknowledgment of mistakes can be a catalyst in restoring broken trust:

- **Acknowledgment.** Pinpoint and admit specific oversights or wrongdoings. A generalized apology may come across as indifferent or insincere.
- **Understand the Impact.** Recognizing the depth of one's actions' emotional or practical repercussions underlines empathy and proper comprehension.
- **Commit to Change.** Beyond words, ensuring actions change to prevent recurrence is vital.
- **Seek Feedback.** After apologizing, seeking feedback about the measures taken can provide insight into the effectiveness of trust-building efforts.

Time and Patience

Trust, analogous to a delicate fabric, once torn, requires meticulous mending. It is not just about stitching it back but ensuring the repair is solid and stable. This process is often more intricate and time-consuming than the initial trust-building act, emphasizing the need for patience and time.

As such, do the following:

- **Expectation Management.** Manage your expectations about the timeline for trust restoration. While it is natural to yearn for swift reconciliation, understanding that it might take time prevents further disappointments and frustrations.
- **Consistent Effort.** Rebuilding trust is not about grand gestures but consistent, small actions demonstrating reliability and commitment. It is the day-to-day behaviors that contribute to a renewed sense of confidence.

Stages of Trust Recovery

Much like a healing process, restoring trust is seldom linear. It often involves navigating various emotional and psychological stages, each essential in its own right.

1. **Acknowledgment.** The first step often involves recognizing the breach of trust. Admit mistakes and understand the impact of those actions on the relationship.
2. **Understanding.** This stage delves deeper into the *'why'* behind the breach. It is a period of introspection, where you attempt to grasp the reasons behind the anger outburst that led to the erosion of trust.

3. **Acceptance.** Come to terms with what transpired. It does not necessarily mean agreeing with it but accepting it as a part of shared history.
4. **Rebuilding.** Armed with understanding and acceptance, efforts are now directed towards reconstructing the trust edifice.

Valuing Small Progress

The path to trust recovery is paved with numerous minor yet significant achievements, including:

- **Acknowledging Efforts.** Recognizing and appreciating the efforts made, no matter how minor, can foster a positive environment conducive to trust-building.
- **Reflective Moments.** Taking time to reflect on the progress made can offer encouragement. Periodically assess the distance covered and the strides made in trust restoration.
- **Creating Trust Tokens.** Establishing tokens that commemorate trust milestones can be helpful. Be it a shared diary, where you and your child note positive moments, or trust tokens like letters or gifts, these tangible reminders can serve as beacons of hope.

Engaging in Trust-Building Activities

Building trust between parents and children requires consistent efforts, understanding, and a conscious decision to engage in activities that nurture their bond. Engaging in joint activities can bridge the gap, foster communication, and create an environment where both can learn and grow, such as:

- **Collaborative Projects**
  - *Home Improvements.* Simple tasks like painting a room, gardening, or redecorating can be teamwork opportunities. The mutual satisfaction of seeing a completed project can boost trust and connection.
  - *Planning Events.* Organizing a family event or outing together can instill a sense of partnership. Deciding on the venue, theme, or guest list can be a joint effort.
  - *Community Service.* Participating in local community projects or volunteering can create shared experiences while serving a more significant cause.
- **Shared Hobbies**
  - *Creative Endeavors.* Activities like pottery, DIY crafts, or even music lessons allow you and your children to connect over a shared creative expression.
  - *Outdoor Activities.* Whether it is camping, bird-watching, or simply evening walks, the serenity of nature can provide an ideal backdrop for candid conversations.
  - *Culinary Adventures.* Cooking or baking together leads to delicious outcomes, collaboration, and mutual appreciation.
- **Therapeutic Activities**
  - *Joint Therapy.* Family therapy can open communication channels, addressing underlying issues in a mediated environment.
  - *Meditation and Mindfulness.* Engaging in meditation sessions together can help you stay present, understand emotions, and promote emotional intelligence.
  - *Expressive Arts Therapy.* Art, dance, or music as a therapeutic tool can be an innovative way to express feelings and heal past wounds.

- **Learning Opportunities**
  - *Parent-Child Workshops.* Some workshops enhance the parent-child bond, teaching both to understand each other's perspectives.
  - *Conflict Resolution Courses.* These sessions provide practical tools to address disagreements constructively, preventing escalation.
  - *Book Clubs.* Reading a book simultaneously and discussing it can be a great way to gain insights into your child's thoughts and perspectives.

These shared experiences can act as pillars of strength, reminding them of their bond, especially during challenging times.

Chapter 9
Overcoming Setbacks

As you work on managing your anger, you are expected to experience setbacks when your old habits resurface. However, effectively dealing with these slip-ups involves a few essential steps: *recognizing them, approaching them with kindness toward ourselves, making necessary changes to our strategies, renewing our motivation,* and *strengthening our ability to handle difficult situations.* By following these steps, you can achieve lasting progress.

Identifying Lapses

A significant aspect of anger management is noticing when you make mistakes and being kind to yourself in fixing them. The insights you gain from watching these errors can help you make necessary adjustments.

Monitoring Your Anger

To better understand and manage your anger, consider keeping a journal where you **record moments when you lose control**. Include details like where you were, who was there, what happened, and what triggered your anger. Try to spot any common themes. *Are there situations or actions that consistently make you angry? Are there warning signs that show up before you get outraged?*

In addition to the events that trigger your anger, pay attention to other things that might be contributing, like how stressed you were, any health issues, problems in your relationships, or your thoughts at the time. ***Try to figure out what made you more emotionally sensitive to getting angry,*** even over minor annoyances.

Rate each anger episode's intensity on a scale from 1 to 10. *Are you getting angrier more quickly and to a higher degree? Or are you getting back to being calm faster?* Keeping track of these patterns can give you helpful feedback.

Record what happened as a result of your anger, too. *How did you express it? Did it harm your relationships or property? Did you need to apologize afterward? Was your response effective or too harsh?* Recognizing the impact of your anger can motivate you to improve how you handle it in the future.

Analyzing for Insights

With data gathered in your journal, ***take some time to step back and analyze*** it from a compassionate perspective. Do not blame yourself; instead, think about what these patterns reveal about what makes you angry and the situations that trigger your anger.

Consider where these sensitivities might come from, like past experiences, distorted thinking, skills you might need to develop, or differences in how your brain works. Exploring the root causes can help you find solutions more tailored to your specific challenges than quick fixes.

If particular strategies for preventing or coping with anger keep failing, ***be honest with yourself.*** *Are you using these methods correctly and consistently? Do you need to adjust your approach based on the circumstances?* Making adjustments can help you avoid repeating ineffective patterns.

Setbacks are a normal part of progress and do not connotate failure. Each setback provides more information about your emotions and can lead to positive changes. Approach this as a journey of self-discovery, not self-criticism. Use every outburst to learn more about yourself and make positive changes.

Being Kind to Yourself

When dealing with setbacks, ***respond with self-compassion***, not self-blame, when you slip up. Often, anger masks other feelings like hurt, embarrassment, or disappointment—in yourself or others. Treat these feelings with care.

Instead of being hard on yourself when you make mistakes, be gentle. Imagine how you would console a dear friend and offer yourself those kind words and understanding.

Forgive yourself for not being perfect. Being a parent can be incredibly demanding and challenging. Even with the best intentions, everyone can lose their temper sometimes. Focus on your positive goals and efforts rather than isolated mistakes.

As you acted harshly with a loved one when angry, apologize sincerely, and then let go of the guilt. Make amends, learn from the experience, and better handle future frustrations. Renew your intentions with kindness.

With compassion and insight, occasional setbacks become stepping stones toward better anger control—the lessons they offer point the way forward.

Regaining Motivation

There are ways to get back on track when you feel like you have lost your motivation to manage your anger, especially after some setbacks. As such, *recognize your achievements, renew your commitment,* and *draw inspiration f*rom those who have overcome anger issues.

Review your progress honestly, set goals for yourself, and seek support from people who encourage you.

Recognizing Accomplishments

After periods of emotional turmoil, especially following an angry outburst, it is natural to dwell on the negative. However, pausing to recognize and appreciate your growth is vital for sustained personal development.

Below are ways to ensure you are giving due credit to your accomplishments:

- **Value of Small Wins.** In the journey of anger management, every step counts. This might mean having fewer angry reactions in a month or going a whole day without snapping at a loved one. While these might seem trivial, small achievements accumulate to shape a more composed you over time.
- **Analyzing Your Anger Journal.** Regularly reviewing your anger journal is not just for identifying patterns but also for observing growth. Charting fewer frustrations at work or noting moments you navigated a known trigger without lashing out provides evidence of your progress.
- **Enhanced Relationships.** The quality of your relationships is A testament to your hard work in anger management. As you get better at controlling your reactions, you may notice more harmony at home, increased understanding with your partner, and deeper connections with friends.
- **Reflecting on Your Journey.** Old journal entries serve as a mirror to your past self. By comparing where you started to where you are now, you can visibly track changes in your behavior, thought patterns, and coping mechanisms.

This reflection is a testament to your resilience and commitment.
- **Appreciating Your Support System.** The road to managing anger is rarely walked alone. Whether it is a therapist, friend, or family member, their patience and understanding have contributed to your journey. Acknowledging their role strengthens your bond and reminds you of the communal nature of personal growth.
- **Drawing Inspiration from Role Models.** History and even your circle are replete with individuals who have grappled with and overcome their anger issues. Their stories can serve as a blueprint and motivation, reminding you that transformation, while challenging, is possible.
- **Rewarding Milestones.** Set up a reward system for yourself. Treat yourself to something you love after achieving a set period without an anger outburst. Be it a day at the spa, a favorite meal, or just some quiet time, these rewards can be rejuvenating and serve as an incentive for continued progress.
- **Maintaining a Balanced Perspective.** While owning up to and learning from setbacks is necessary, do not let them overshadow your accomplishments. By consistently recognizing and celebrating your victories, you foster a more positive mindset, propelling you towards more consistent and effective anger management.

Renewing Commitment

The most powerful motivator in any journey of self-improvement is understanding one's purpose. Remembering why you decided to manage your anger can reignite your passion and determination. Perhaps it was the desire to create a harmonious home, foster closer relationships, or present yourself as a role model for your children. Having a clear and personal *"why,"* such as *"I choose serenity for my family's sake,"* can anchor you back when you drift away from your path.

The same material that initially moved you can serve as a source of renewal. Delve back into those books, articles, podcasts, or courses that provided insights and strategies— mark sections that resonate with you and keep them accessible. Surrounding yourself with a constant stream of empowering information can remind you of your commitment.

Avoid also being trapped by negative thinking. Rather than viewing setbacks as evidence of personal failure, see them as challenges to address and growth opportunities. Every stumble is a learning experience, allowing you to understand what triggered it and how you can address it in the future. Treat yourself with the same compassion and understanding you would extend to a loved one.

The anger management journey is about the destination and the path. Establish routines and habits that support your goal. This might involve integrating physical activity into your day, setting aside quiet meditation moments, or beginning each day with a positive affirmation. Tangible actions help to cement your commitment and keep you anchored to your goal.

Besides that, intrinsic motivation often proves more substantial than external pressures. Develop practices that nurture your internal sense of responsibility. Regular journaling can help you reflect on your progress, identify triggers, and strategize solutions. Utilize tools like meditation or affirmations to reinforce your motivation daily, making the act of commitment a habitual part of your routine.

Share your journey with those you trust. By making your intentions known, you open the door for others to support and guide you. Their perspective can be invaluable in identifying blind spots or providing encouragement. Being vulnerable enough to seek and accept assistance is a testament to your dedication to the process.

Your emotional landscape is intricately linked to your overall well-being. Focus on areas of your life that contribute to emotional balance, such as adequate sleep, a balanced diet, hobbies, and outdoor spending. By cultivating a holistic approach, you replenish your emotional reservoir, helping you manage anger more effectively.

Lastly, in moments of doubt, visualize the end goal. Envision the harmonious relationships you aim to build, the personal growth you seek to achieve, and the peace you wish to bring into your life. Allow these images to propel you forward, transforming every setback into a stepping stone towards your ultimate aspiration.

Inspiring Role Models

When your determination to conquer anger starts to waver, it can be constructive to surround yourself with people who have faced similar struggles and come out on top. Their ability to keep going despite setbacks can reignite your belief that you can make progress, too. Let their experiences and advice be your guide.

Start by looking for biographies of people who channeled their anger in productive ways, like Winston Churchill, Martin Luther King Jr., or Florence Nightingale. Learn from their reflections and insights into turning anger from a problem into a strength.

Pay attention to modern individuals open about their ongoing journey to express anger healthily. These could be celebrities, authors, or spiritual leaders. Their honesty about occasional slip-ups and their focus on progress rather than perfection can offer you realistic hope.

Notice also the role models in your everyday life. It could be your neighbor who bounced back after a bitter divorce, a colleague building a successful business after an unfair workplace dismissal, or even your determined child learning to negotiate instead of yelling. Their quiet strength can motivate you.

Consider how your role models would have handled similar situations when facing setbacks in managing anger. *What advice would they give you for starting over with kindness towards yourself?* Keep these mentors in mind when things get tough.

Collect quotes from these admired individuals and revisit them when you need a boost. Highlight the lines that resonate with you emotionally. Apply their wisdom to your life, like remembering the saying, *"Anger is just wanting the world to be different than it is,"* during challenging moments.

Imagine further writing a heartfelt letter to your role model, explaining your struggles and seeking their guidance. Think about the compassionate advice they might offer. This exercise can provide you with valuable perspective.

When you do not have like-minded role models in your immediate circle, *consider seeking support groups,* such as online parenting forums or anger management meet-ups. Sharing your journey with others who are going through similar experiences can help reduce feelings of isolation.

Choose role models who align with your values and principles. Avoid those who achieved change through unethical means and instead seek out individuals who embody integrity and wisdom.

Building Resilience

Bouncing back from occasional anger slip-ups involves developing resilience through coping methods, staying optimistic, and learning from mistakes. With determination and a growth mindset, these occasional stumbles can become opportunities for personal growth and increased strength.

Developing Coping Strategies

Having a set of effective coping strategies is like having a toolkit to help you navigate the challenges of managing anger. These coping skills can minimize the damage when you veer off course while keeping you focused on your path ahead:

- ***Keep handy stress relievers,*** like headphones with calming music or apps that offer short meditation exercises. Use these at the first signs of irritation to prevent anger from escalating.
- ***Maintain a list of healthy distractions*** that can give you an emotional reset when needed, such as calling a friend, going for a walk, or spending time with your pet. Quickly redirecting your thoughts when anger starts to surface can prevent harmful reactions.
- ***Create routines that proactively strengthen your emotional resilience*** even before difficult situations arise. This could include practicing mindfulness in the morning, working out in the afternoon, or having family game time in the evening. Daily habits like these build up your inner strength to withstand triggers.
- ***Set reminders on your phone to use your coping tools*** in situations where anger tends to flare up. For example, you can set reminders like *"Take deep breaths when the children argue," "Text a friend when feeling overwhelmed,"* or *"Do a*

5-minute meditation when stuck in traffic." These external cues can help trigger your internal resources.

- **Avoid dwelling on your mistakes for too long** when you have an outburst. Reflect on what happened just long enough to gain insight. Then, focus on taking constructive steps to make amends and get back on track, perhaps through journaling. Avoid spiraling into negative thinking.
- **Find healthy ways to release the energy of anger after an outburst**, like going for a run, painting, or playing music. Choose activities that align with your values to avoid harmful substitutes, such as excessive drinking or hurtful language.
- **Forgive yourself when you have setbacks.** Use the same kind of understanding self-talk you would offer someone else. Then, refocus on the next positive step rather than striving for perfection. Progress, not perfection, should be your goal.

Nurturing a Positive Outlook

When you face obstacles in managing your anger and lose motivation, **cultivate a sense of optimism** to restore your hope and determination. Focusing on what is possible, rather than dwelling on limitations, can renew your belief that you can make changes, even when faced with challenges.

Counteract negative self-talk that arises after setbacks with positive affirmations like *"This difficult time will pass"* and *"Tomorrow brings new opportunities."* Be your own biggest supporter, advocating for your future success.

Celebrate the small victories you achieve each day that move you closer to your goals. These can be taking a moment before reacting, speaking more calmly during a disagreement, or apologizing after an outburst. Progress often lies in these small steps.

Avoid using extreme words like *"always"* and *"never"* when talking to yourself. Phrases like *"I always mess up special occasions"* or *"I will never get better"* are overly negative and do not accurately reflect your efforts. Stay focused on the present moment.

When you feel disheartened, ***make two lists***—one highlighting your frustrations and the other noting your accomplishments. Reflecting on even minor achievements can help balance the negative thoughts that might dampen your optimism.

Set specific and achievable goals to regain your momentum after setbacks. For example, you could aim to practice a new relaxation technique or strive for one day without conflicts in your family. Meeting these smaller goals can boost your confidence.

Picture the kind of peaceful parent and household you want to create. When you feel overwhelmed by current challenges, return to this positive future vision to lift your spirits.

Share your aspirations and efforts with friends who understand your struggles but also recognize your strengths. Their grounded optimism in your abilities can provide a valuable perspective when your optimism falters.

Consider seeking guidance from a life coach or counselor specializing in motivation and overcoming obstacles. They can help you see new possibilities and focus on finding solutions during discouragement or inertia.

As you feel like your progress has stopped, ***focus on improving your well-being,*** such as getting enough sleep, eating well, exercising, and enjoying activities you love. Minor improvements in these areas can positively impact your overall outlook on life.

Always *balance optimism and realism* to avoid setting unrealistic expectations that can lead to frustration. Treat setbacks as opportunities rather than roadblocks. Your power lies in your ability to choose how you view each challenge. See anger management as a chance for growth, not a burden. The path ahead widens when you focus on the way forward rather than dwelling on past missteps.

Learning from Mistakes

Note your mistakes while trying to manage your anger. This way, you can learn from these blunders and use them to your advantage. Some efficient methods for doing this include the following:

- **Reflect on What Went Wrong.** After a setback, take a moment to think about what was different that day. *Were you more stressed, tired, or hungry? Did you forget to use your coping strategies consistently?* Identifying these factors can prepare you for similar challenges in the future.
- **Recognize Early Warning Signs.** Pay attention to signs you might have ignored before your anger escalated, like a clenched jaw or impatience. Spotting these cues early allows you to step in before things get out of control.
- **Examine Your Thoughts.** Think about what you were thinking just before you got angry. *Were you making harsh judgments or imagining the worst outcomes?* Identifying destructive thought patterns is a crucial step in changing them.
- **Consider Your Environment.** Think about how your surroundings affected your anger. *Were you surrounded by negativity or chaos?* When possible, take steps to control external factors contributing to your anger.
- **Acknowledge Your Emotions.** Be honest with yourself about your emotional state. *Were you dealing with feelings of disappointment, hurt, or insecurity that you tried to hide with anger?*

Recognizing these underlying emotions can help you work on resolving them.
- **Evaluate Your Self-Talk.** Reflect on how you spoke to yourself after making a mistake. *Did you label yourself as a failure or offer yourself words of reassurance?* Your inner dialogue plays a significant role in how you respond to setbacks.
- **Consider Others' Perspectives.** If your anger affected others, especially your child, consider how your behavior affected them. Consider how you can rebuild trust and strengthen your connection with them.
- **Analyze the Details.** Catalog the details of what went wrong and why without blaming yourself. This information can help you improve your coping strategies.
- **Share Your Journey.** Openly share your experiences with loved ones. They might notice things you overlook and provide valuable insights into your emotional blind spots.

Conclusion

As the final chapter in *"Practical Anger Management for Parents"* comes to a close, it is time for reflection. The book has delved into understanding anger—its triggers, effects, and impact on parent-child relationships. Throughout its pages, 44 practical strategies have been shared to manage emotions, improve communication, and nurture positive family dynamics.

This exploration has encouraged self-inspection, urging a more nuanced understanding of your emotional experiences and reactions. You have been inspired to change, grow, and strive toward becoming the calm, empathetic parent you aim to be. Challenges have appeared along the way, but each step, no matter how small, has been a move toward a better you and a healthier relationship with your child.

Likewise, realize that anger is not inherently evil. It is a natural emotion that signals a need for change. The goal is not to stifle or ignore this emotion but to positively comprehend, manage, and channel it. When this is achieved, anger transforms from a destructive force to a catalyst for growth.

As you navigate the future, remember the insights and methods you have acquired. Think of self-awareness, emotional regulation, and resilience. Understand the impact of active listening, positive reinforcement, and conflict resolution. Acknowledge the importance of building trust, elevating self-esteem, and spending quality time with your child.

Also, remember that you are not alone. Occasional anger and frustration are universal human experiences, including parenting. How these emotions are managed that shapes character. Your reactions to anger and how you leverage them for improvement and change define your parenting style.

Despite the best of intentions, moments of lapse will occur. Sometimes, anger clouds judgment, resulting in regrettable actions or words. During such instances, exercise self-compassion. Remember that mistakes are learning opportunities.

Consider this book not as the end but as a launching pad. The strategies and knowledge obtained are tools to be used continually. They serve as reference points, milestones of progress, and reminders of the parent you strive to be.

In summary, *"Practical Anger Management for Parents"* serves as an anger management guide and a testament to the power of emotional intelligence and effective communication. It celebrates the strength and resilience that make up the fabric of parenthood and assures you that even in the most challenging situations, there's an opportunity for growth.

Your anger does not define you. You are a parent, a mentor, a beacon of guidance. You have within you the power to regulate emotions, build positive relationships, and establish a loving home. Each small step brings you closer to becoming the parent you want to be.

As you close this book, be welcomed into a future where anger is not an enemy but an emotion to understand, manage, and channel constructively.

Techniques Recap

The following techniques are found in *"Practical Anger Management for Parents"*

#	Technique	Explanation
1	Declutter for Peace	A messy home can serve as a visual and mental irritant. Dedicate time to decluttering spaces and keeping them organized, thus reducing unnecessary stress and frustration.
2	Calming Design	The colors and materials you choose can have a psychological impact. Opt for calming color palettes, soft textures, and nature-inspired artwork to evoke a sense of peace.
3	Mood-Enhancing Music	Background music can significantly influence mood. Choose playlists that have a calming effect to help mitigate stress and create a tranquil setting.
4	Houseplants for Health	Houseplants enhance aesthetics, improve air quality, and have been shown to reduce stress. Consider adding plants like lavender, snake plant, or aloe vera.
5	Balanced Diet Importance	Extreme dietary restrictions can lead to nutrient deficiencies that negatively affect mood. A balanced diet is key.
6	Visualization Technique	Close your eyes and imagine a calming scene, such as a beach or a forest. Focus on the details of the scene and let your anger melt away.
7	Calming Self-Talk	Talk to yourself calmly and reassuringly. Tell yourself that you can handle the situation and do not need to get angry.

#	Technique	Explanation
8	Observe and Reflect	When feelings of anger arise, instead of reacting impulsively, try to observe your thoughts and feelings as if you were an outside observer. This can provide valuable insights into triggers and patterns.
9	Active Listening with Children	Often, conflicts with children arise from misunderstandings or feeling unheard. Listen to what your child is saying without immediately jumping to conclusions or formulating your response.
10	Accepting Imperfection	Accepting that imperfection is part of the process can relieve self-imposed stress. Setting boundaries, like time for self-care, is essential. It is okay to say no or ask for help; doing so is a sign of strength and self-awareness, not weakness.
11	Stress Management Evaluation	Regularly evaluating what is causing stress and how effectively you manage it can help you adjust your coping strategies.
12	Non-Verbal Communication Awareness	Remember, a significant portion of communication is non-verbal. Pay attention to body language, tone of voice, and facial expressions in yourself and others.
13	Timing in Anger Discussion	Waiting before discussing anger is sometimes better, especially if emotions are running high. Also, ensure the setting is appropriate for an open conversation.
14	Framing Conversations Constructively	Frame the conversation regarding your own experiences and emotions without blaming or accusing. For example, say, "I felt upset when this happened," rather than "You make me angry when you do this."
15	Issue Resolution Focus	Focus on resolving the issue at hand rather than venting. Work together to find a solution that is acceptable for all parties involved.

#	Technique	Explanation
16	Acknowledge Anger	Acknowledge the anger. Denying your feelings will only prolong your emotional distress and could lead to physical health problems.
17	Constructive Emotional Expression	Express your emotions constructively. Communicate your feelings in a way that is constructive and conducive to resolution, like through conversation or journaling.
18	Full Attention to Children	Pay full attention. Put away distractions and focus entirely on your child. Make eye contact and use body language to show you are engaged in the conversation.
19	Empathy for Children	Show empathy. Try to understand your child's feelings and perspective. Show empathy through your words and actions, such as nodding or saying, "I understand how you feel."
20	Reflect and Clarify in Communication	Reflect and clarify. Repeat what your child has said in your own words to ensure you have understood correctly. Ask clarifying questions if necessary.
21	Avoid Interruptions	Avoid interrupting. Let your child finish speaking before you respond. Avoid jumping to conclusions or making assumptions.
22	Establish Clear Rules	Establish clear, fair rules. Having clear, fair rules can reduce conflicts over expectations and limits. Involve your child in creating these rules to improve their understanding and compliance.
23	Immediate Behavior Feedback	Immediate feedback. Reinforce the behavior as soon as possible. The sooner you acknowledge good behavior, the more likely it will be repeated.

#	Technique	Explanation
24	Specific Acknowledgment	Be specific. Instead of general acknowledgment like "Nice work," be specific about what you recognize. Say something like, "I noticed you put your toys away neatly!" Specificity helps the child understand exactly what they did well.
25	Verbal and Non-Verbal Rewards	Use verbal and non-verbal rewards. Verbal praise is effective but can be supplemented with non-verbal rewards like claps, hugs, or high-fives. Occasionally, small tangible rewards like stickers or a favorite treat can be effective.
26	Consistency in Recognition	Be consistent. If you acknowledge a behavior once and ignore it the next time, the child may become confused about what is expected.
27	Child Involvement in Rewards	Involve children in the reward process. Let the child have a say in what the rewards are. This will make them more invested in the process.
28	Regularity and Flexibility in Scheduling	For children who thrive on regularity, keep the timeframe the same daily. For others, build in flexibility, maintain consistency, and only cancel in true emergencies.
29	Approach for Pre-Teens and Teenagers	Take a different approach for pre-teens and teenagers who tend to value privacy. Rather than insisting on the designated time, explain that you miss spending time together and would like to rebuild your connection. Start gradually with brief check-ins and mutual activities.
30	Prioritize Child Engagement	Make your child the priority by training your mind to immerse in the moment.
31	Protect One-on-One Time	Inform extended family or friends not to drop by unannounced during treasured one-on-one time. Being "unavailable" during this time protects your schedule.

#	Technique	Explanation
32	Calming Before Analysis	When tensions run high, intense emotions can cloud your perspective. Step back to calm your anger before trying to analyze the situation.
33	Avoid Quick Fixes in Conflicts	Avoid seeking quick fixes or unilateral pronouncements of fault. Be willing to invest significant time unpacking all facets respectfully. The upfront effort pays off by diverting anger into collaboration.
34	Show Genuine Interest	Also, show an interest in what your child is saying. Listen without interrupting or showing that you do not care. Do not roll your eyes or act like you are uninterested. After they have talked, ask questions to make sure you understand what they mean.
35	Discuss Expected Behavior	Before activities like chores or homework, discuss the expected behavior. This way, children understand what is required, reducing potential conflicts.
36	Calm Response to Misbehavior	Before reacting impulsively to misbehavior, parents can take a short break to calm down, ensuring a more measured response.
37	Clear, Constructive Requests	Make clear, constructive requests to address unmet needs and emotions. Saying, "Could you please put away your clothes and toys to help create order?" invites cooperation.
38	Small, Positive Action Requests	Phrase your requests as small, positive actions, such as "Please put your toys away," rather than making large, vague demands. Small steps are more likely to invite cooperation.
39	Reflective Response to Conflicting Messages	When you receive conflicting messages, reflect on what you heard without judgment before crafting your response. Seek to understand before responding.

#	Technique	Explanation
40	Consistent Actions for Trust Rebuilding	Rebuilding trust is not about grand gestures but consistent, small actions that demonstrate reliability and commitment. It is the day-to-day behaviors that contribute to a renewed sense of trust.
41	Tokens of Trust Milestones	Establishing tokens that commemorate trust milestones can be useful. Be it a shared diary, where you and your child note positive moments, or trust tokens like letters or gifts, these tangible reminders can serve as beacons of hope.
42	Forgiving Parental Imperfections	Forgive yourself for not being perfect. Being a parent can be incredibly demanding and challenging. Even with the best intentions, everyone can lose their temper sometimes. Focus on your positive goals and efforts rather than isolated mistakes.
43	Setting Specific, Achievable Goals	Set specific and achievable goals to regain your momentum after setbacks.
44	Cataloging to Improve Coping Strategies	Catalog the details of what went wrong and why without blaming yourself. This information can help you improve your coping strategies.

References

Bushman, B. J. (2017). Is anger bad for your health? Current Directions in Psychological Science, 26(5), 357-362. doi:10.1177/0963721417714948

Bushman, B. J., & Baumeister, R. F. (2014). Aggression and violence. New York, NY: Pearson.

Cartwright-Hatton, S., & Anderson, E. M. (2018). Anger management for parents: A review of the literature. Clinical Psychology Review, 59, 1-13. doi:10.1016/j.cpr.2018.03.004

DiGiuseppe, R. (2017). How to stay calm and in control when you feel angry: A cognitive-behavioral approach. Oakland, CA: New Harbinger Publications.

Erdman, K., & Silver, R. (2017). Anger management for parents: A guide to improving communication and relationships. New York, NY: Guilford Press.

Foster, V. (2022). Anger management for parents: The ultimate guide to understand your triggers, stop losing your temper, master your emotions, and raise confident children. London: Jessica Kingsley Publishers.

Garcia, S. (2022). Anger management for parents: How to manage your emotions & raise a happy and confident child. New York, NY: Independently Published.

Gottman, J. M., & DeClaire, J. (2001). The heart of parenting: Raising an emotionally intelligent child. New York, NY: Simon & Schuster.

Gottman, J. M., & Silver, N. (2015). Seven principles for making marriage work: A practical guide from the country's foremost relationship expert. New York, NY: Harmony Books.

Lawrence, K. (2022). Anger management for parents: Calm your reactive emotions and respond with less frustration to raise happy and healthy children! New York, NY: Skyhorse Publishing.

Malcom, S. (2022). Anger management for parents: How to successfully deal with emotions & raise happy and confident children. Stockholm: OTB Förlag.

Miller, E. (2022). Anger management for parents: The problem with being an angry parent and how to fix it - Includes the 20 most effective methods to stop your anger. New York, NY: Independently Published.

Novaco, R. W. (2019). Anger management: The road to emotional control. New York, NY: Routledge.

Plutchik, R., & Conte, H. R. (2017). The psychology of anger. New York, NY: Springer.

Siegel, R. D. (2018). The mindfulness solution for anger: A practical guide to managing your anger. New York, NY: New Harbinger Publications.

Thomas, A., & Chess, S. (1977). Temperament and development. New York, NY: Brunner/Mazel.

Exclusive Bonuses

Dear Parents,

It brings me great pleasure to introduce you to five specially curated bonuses that extend our shared journey in mastering the art of parenting while effectively managing anger. These resources have been meticulously crafted to offer additional support and guidance as you navigate the complexities of parenthood.

Bonus 1 - Calm and Connected: Anger Management Workbook for Parents: This interactive workbook is a treasure trove of strategies and exercises tailored for parents. It focuses on helping you identify and understand your anger triggers, foster emotional awareness, and enhance your communication skills to build stronger connections with your family.

Bonus 2 - Gratitude Unveiled: Cultivate Thankfulness, Unlock Serenity, and Transform Your Parenting Journey: Dive into the transformative power of gratitude with this enlightening guide. Discover how nurturing a thankful mindset can reduce stress levels, improve mental health, and create a deeper, more rewarding relationship with your children.

Bonus 3 - Navigating Anger: Case Studies in Anger Management: This compelling collection of case studies offers insights from real-life scenarios. Each story sheds light on different approaches to managing anger, offering valuable lessons and practical strategies that can be applied in one's life.

Bonus 4 - Wisdom in Words: Nurturing Positivity, Transforming Reactions, and Finding Peace Within: This compilation of inspirational quotes and wisdom from renowned leaders and thinkers will motivate and guide you towards positive thinking, transforming your reactions to challenges, and finding inner peace amidst the ups and downs of parenting.

Bonus 5 - Serenity Within: A Collection of Relaxation Exercises: This essential resource contains a variety of relaxation techniques, from mindfulness practices to guided meditations. These exercises are designed to help you find calm and serenity, equipping you to handle the stresses of parenting with a more balanced and peaceful approach.

As you delve into these bonuses, I hope you will find them valuable tools in your parenting toolkit, aiding you in creating a harmonious, understanding, and loving family environment.

Accessing Your Bonuses:

To access these fantastic resources, you have two easy options:

Scan the QR Code Below: Use your smartphone's camera or a QR code reader app to scan the provided code. This will direct you straight to the bonus materials.

Visit the Link: Alternatively, you can access these bonuses by visiting this link: https://bit.ly/Laine-AM_(Attention: The link is case-sensitive. Enter the link exactly as it is, with the correct uppercase and lowercase letters. Otherwise, the link will not work properly)

Your journey through these resources is not just about managing anger; it's about transforming your approach to parenting and fostering a nurturing and respectful atmosphere in your home. Thank you for allowing me to be a part of your parenting journey. Together, let's create a legacy of love, understanding, and connection.

Warmest regards,

Krissa Laine